NOT YOUR USUAL *Workbook*

GRADE 3

fast + est = fastest

63 ÷ 9 = 7

SUPPORTS • SUPPORTS • Current State Standards • SUPPORTS • SUPPORTS

D1398754

Thinking Kids®
Carson-Dellosa Publishing LLC
Greensboro, North Carolina

Thinking Kids®
Carson-Dellosa Publishing LLC
P.O. Box 35665
Greensboro, NC 27425 USA

© 2017 Carson-Dellosa Publishing LLC. Except as permitted under the United States Copyright Act, no part of this publication may be reproduced, stored, or distributed in any form or by any means (mechanically, electronically, recording, etc.) without the prior written consent of Carson-Dellosa Publishing LLC. Thinking Kids® is an imprint of Carson-Dellosa Publishing LLC.

Printed in the USA • All rights reserved.
01-335167784

ISBN 978-1-4838-3494-8

Contents

Awesome Activities for Practicing Math Skills

Awesome Activities for Practicing Language Arts Skills

Draw a line to match each number (in a fish) to the nearest 100 (in the seaweed).

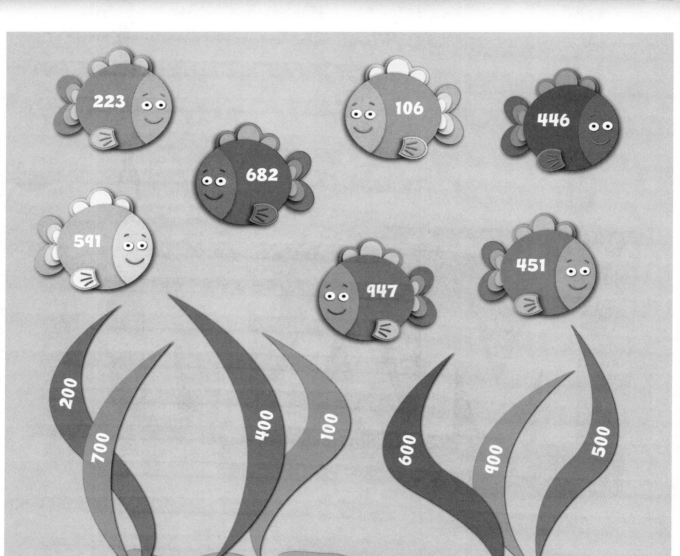

Picture Perfect!

1. $100 - 88 =$ **12**

2. $29 + 30 =$ **59**

3. $17 - 7 =$ **10**

4. $22 - 11 =$ **11**

5. $85 - 6 =$ **79**

6. $35 + 16 =$ **51**

7. $52 - 10 =$ **42**

8. $14 + 14 =$ **28**

9. $66 - 33 =$ **33**

10. $24 + 16 =$ **40**

ON THE DOT

Skills: Addition, Subtraction

Solve the equations. Connect the dots in the order of your answers. Color the picture.

A quadrilateral is a shape with four sides. Follow each set of drawing directions. Turn each shape into a picture of something you like.

DRAW

QUICK

Draw a quadrilateral that is the shape of something you might fly on a windy day.

Draw a quadrilateral that has two sets of parallel sides and no right angles.

Draw a quadrilateral that has four equal sides and four equal angles.

Draw a quadrilateral that has four unequal sides.

Find a secret trail through the forest! Start at 25. Look for a number pattern. Use it to trace a path and find the way out.

Math ↑↓ path

DARE TO DECODE

Use what you know about fractions to crack the code and reveal the secret word.

Secret Word:

1	3	1	1	5	7	3	7

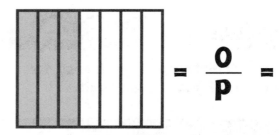

$= \dfrac{R}{O} =$ ☐

$= \dfrac{O}{P} =$ ☐

$= \dfrac{L}{S} =$ ☐

$= \dfrac{R}{I} =$ ☐

IT FITS!

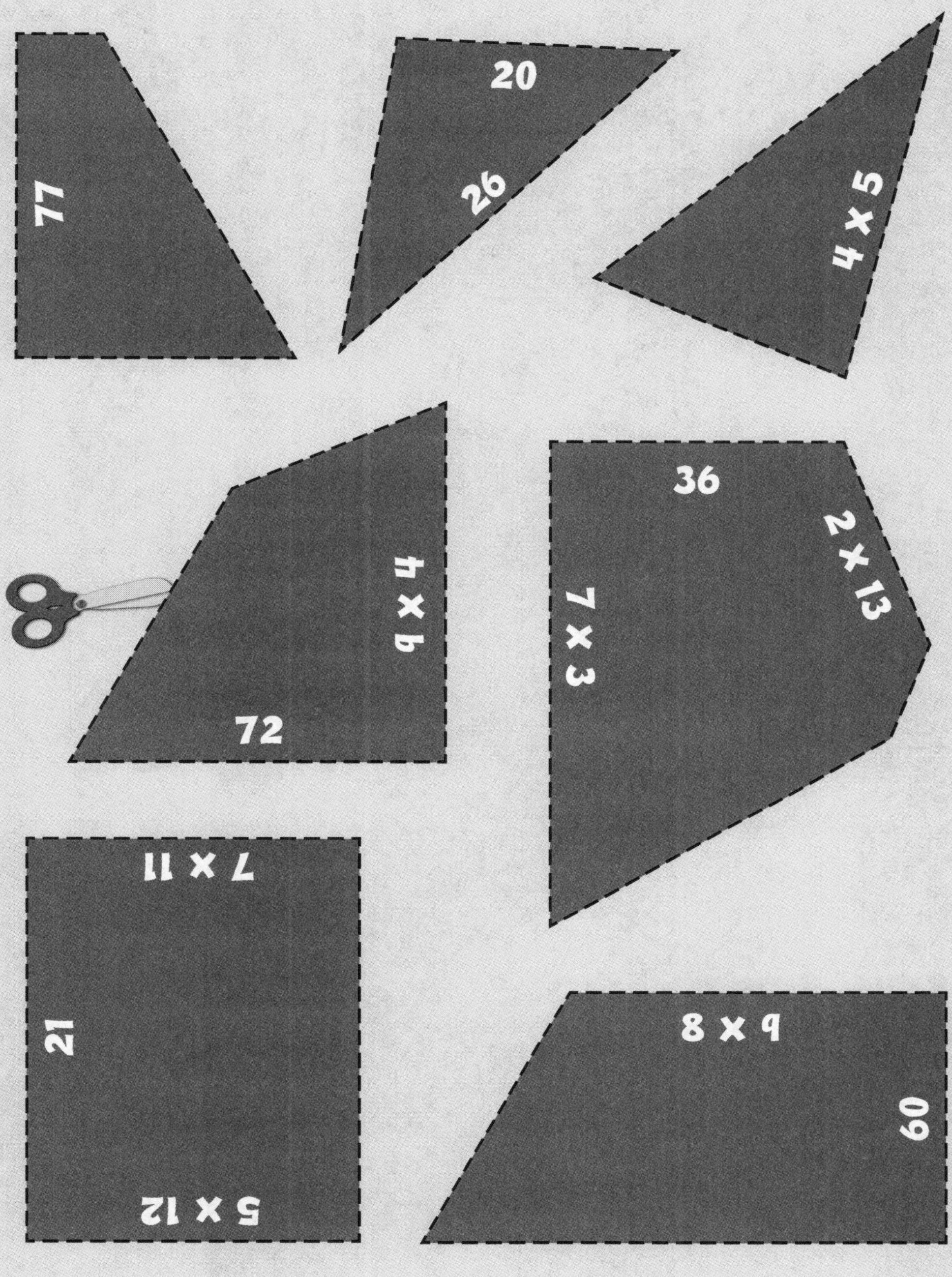

77
20
26
4 × 5
4 × 9
72
36
2 × 13
7 × 3
7 × 11
21
5 × 12
9 × 8
60

What is the mystery shape? ____________________

Skill: Multiplication

Cut out the pieces. Fit them together to form a mystery shape. When the puzzle is solved correctly, each equation and its answer will be next to each other.

GUESS AGAIN

Use each set of clues to discover the mystery number.

It is greater than 3 × 15.

It is less than 8 × 7.

It can be divided evenly by 3.

The sum of its two digits is 6.

The mystery number is ____.

It is less than 80 ÷ 2.

It is an odd number.

It is greater than 3 × 12.

The difference between its two digits is 6.

The mystery number is ____.

Skills: Multiplication, Division, Place Value

Start with the product of 6 × 7.

Switch the digits' places.

Divide the new number by 6.

Add 3.

The mystery number is ____.

Start with the total number of sides of 3 triangles.

Double the number.

Subtract 3.

Multiply by 2.

The mystery number is ____.

Magic Square

The clocks in each row from left to right and in each column from top to bottom show the same amount of time passed. Draw hands on the blank clock faces to solve the puzzle. How much time passed?

☐ hours

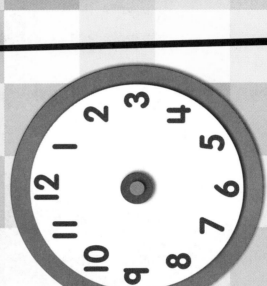

SHAPE MASTER

A quadrilateral is a shape with four sides. How many quadrilaterals can you find in the picture?
I found _____ quadrilaterals

Skill: Quadrilaterals

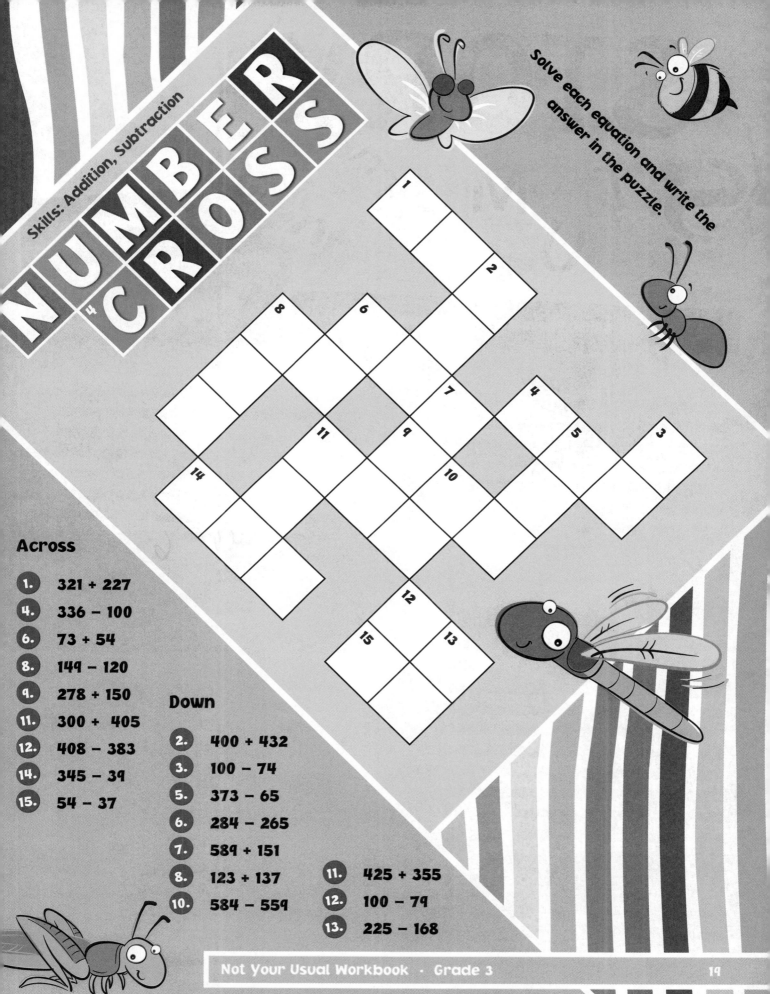

NUMBER CROSS

Skills: Addition, Subtraction

Solve each equation and write the answer in the puzzle.

Across

1. 321 + 227
4. 336 – 100
6. 73 + 54
8. 149 – 120
9. 278 + 150
11. 300 + 405
12. 408 – 383
14. 345 – 39
15. 54 – 37

Down

2. 400 + 432
3. 100 – 74
5. 373 – 65
6. 284 – 265
7. 589 + 151
8. 123 + 137
10. 584 – 559
11. 425 + 355
12. 100 – 79
13. 225 – 168

STORY STUMPERS

Skills: Perimeter, Area, Word Problems

Rex drew a triangle. Its perimeter was 9 inches. Lacey drew a pentagon. Its perimeter was 15 inches. Isabella drew an octagon. Its perimeter was 24 inches. Liam drew a square. What was its perimeter?

_____ inches

Logan went to the lumber store. He bought four 8-foot boards to use for building the sides of a square sandbox. Once he got home, he changed his mind. He now wanted the sandbox to be shaped like an octagon. How long can each side be at most if he does not go back to the lumber store?

_____ feet

Squirrels in Space is a square picture book with sides that measure 30 cm. *Mice from Mars* is a rectangular picture book with a length of 36 cm. The perimeter of the square book is equal to the perimeter of the rectangular book. What is the width of the rectangular book?

_____ centimeters

The rectangular top of a table is 3 times as long as it is wide. Its width is 7 meters. Find the area of the tabletop.

_____ square meters

A Show of Hands

Skill: Picture Graphs

Nell went on a nature walk. Cut out the pictures of creatures she saw. Then, glue or tape them in the columns to make a picture graph. Write a label for each column.

Multiply the number in the center of the flower by the number on each petal.

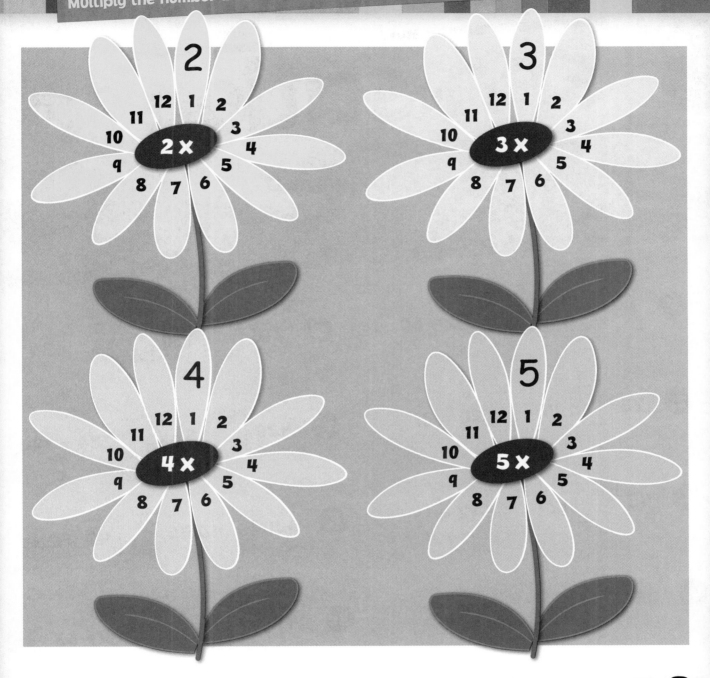

Picture Perfect!

e(quation) sen+sation

Add plus signs (+) and minus signs (−) to make the equations true.

1. 68 ☐+ 65 ☐− 73 = 60

2. 75 ☐8 14 ☐✗ 20 = 81

3. 45 ☐8 127 ☐9 12 = 160

4. 32 ☐5 15 ☐6 27 = 74

5. 58 ☐7 29 ☐9 29 = 116

6. 218 ☐8 150 ☐7 32 = 36

7. 420 ☐50 56 ☐60 220 = 144

8. 300 ☐3 256 ☐6 45 = 511

9. 199 ☐9 47 ☐2 100 = 52

10. 525 ☐7 125 ☐8 300 = 700

PATTERN POWER

Skill: Understanding Fractions

1. $\dfrac{1}{32}$ $\quad$ $\dfrac{1}{16}$ $\quad$ $\dfrac{1}{8}$

2. $\dfrac{1}{3}$ $\quad$ $\dfrac{1}{5}$ $\quad$ $\dfrac{1}{7}$

3. $\dfrac{1}{2}$ $\quad$ $\dfrac{2}{3}$ $\quad$ $\dfrac{3}{4}$

4. $\dfrac{1}{8}$ $\quad$ $\dfrac{2}{8}$ $\quad$ $\dfrac{3}{8}$

5. $\dfrac{10}{10}$ $\quad$ $\dfrac{8}{10}$ $\quad$ $\dfrac{6}{10}$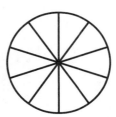

Write the fraction that comes next in each pattern.
Then, color in the circle to show the fraction you wrote.

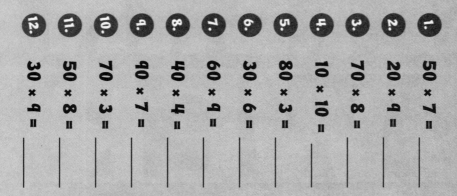

Skill:
Multiples of 10

Solve each equation. Then, find and circle the answers in the puzzle.

1. 50 × 7 = _____
2. 20 × 9 = _____
3. 70 × 8 = _____
4. 10 × 10 = _____
5. 80 × 3 = _____
6. 30 × 6 = _____
7. 60 × 9 = _____
8. 40 × 4 = _____
9. 90 × 7 = _____
10. 70 × 3 = _____
11. 50 × 8 = _____
12. 30 × 9 = _____

3	5	0	2	0	1	3	9	0
5	0	4	3	1	2	0	9	4
1	6	3	2	0	0	7	0	
0	4	0	1	8	1	9	6	0
3	6	0	8	8	3	6	3	7
5	1	3	0	8	0	0	0	7
5	6	8	3	7	2	4	0	4
8	6	1	0	2	7	0	6	1
5	6	3	5	4	0	7	3	3

28

6

19

15

9 **20**   **24**

12

ON THE DOT

Skill: Perimeter

Find the perimeter of each figure. Then, connect the dots in the order of your answers.

1. 3 3
   3
   _____ units

2. 7
   _____ units

3. 2
   4
   _____ units

4. 6 10
   8
   _____ units

5. 1 1 1
   1 1
   1
   _____ units

6. 3
   7 4
   5
   _____ units

7. 3 7
   5
   _____ units

8. 5
   _____ units

DRAW

Skill: Equivalent Fractions

Draw 12 squares. Color $\frac{1}{2}$ of them red and $\frac{1}{2}$ of them blue. Circle 3 red squares. Circle 3 blue squares. Write 2 equivalent fractions that show how many of the squares are circled.

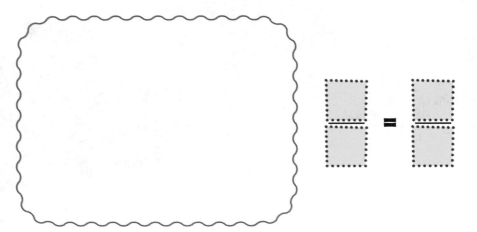

Draw 12 circles. Color $\frac{1}{4}$ of them green. Color the rest of them yellow. Cross out 3 green circles and 5 yellow circles. Write two equivalent fractions that show how many of the yellow circles are not crossed out.

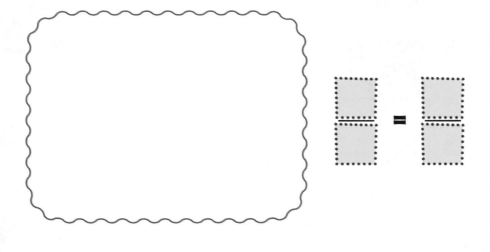

Skill: Comparing Fractions

Cut out the pieces. Match the halves to make the inequalities true. Hint: All pairs will have either the same numerator (top number) or denominator (bottom number).

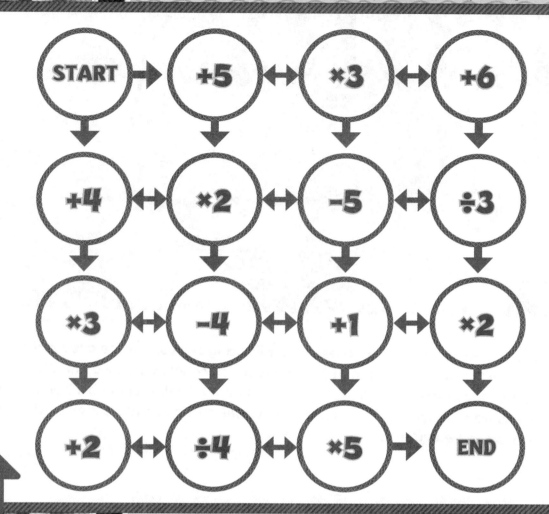

START → +5 ↔ *3 ↔ +6

+4 ↔ *2 ↔ -5 ↔ ÷3

*3 ↔ -4 ↔ +1 ↔ *2

+2 ↔ ÷4 ↔ *5 → END

Can you make your way through the maze and end with 25? Starting with 0, follow the arrows and perform each operation. Keep a running total as you move along. Color in the circles you use. There is only one correct path.

Math path

STORY STUMPERS

Read each problem carefully. Use logic and your math skills to find the answers.

Maya's mother ordered 12 ice cream cones for a birthday party. The ice cream flavors were chocolate, vanilla, strawberry, and bubblegum. There were twice as many chocolate cones as strawberry. There were twice as many vanilla cones as bubblegum. There was one less vanilla cone than strawberry. Label and color the cones to show how many of each flavor were ordered.

Hector has 15 fish in his aquarium. There are 3 times as many yellow fish as striped fish. The number of green fish equals the number of yellow fish plus 1. There are 5 more green fish than striped fish. Label and color the fish to show how many of each type are in Hector's aquarium.

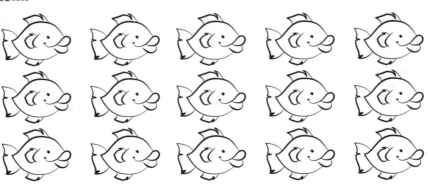

MASTER SHAPES

Cut out the small triangles and squares. Then, arrange them to fill the larger shapes. How many of each small shape did you need to use? Write the number to show the area.

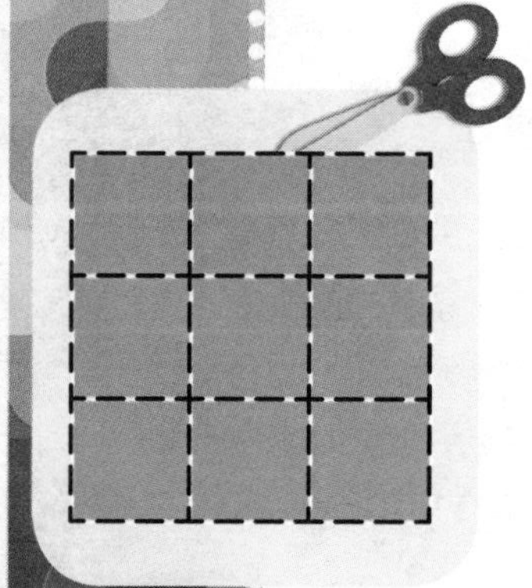

Area = ____ triangles

Area = ____ triangles

Area = ____ squares

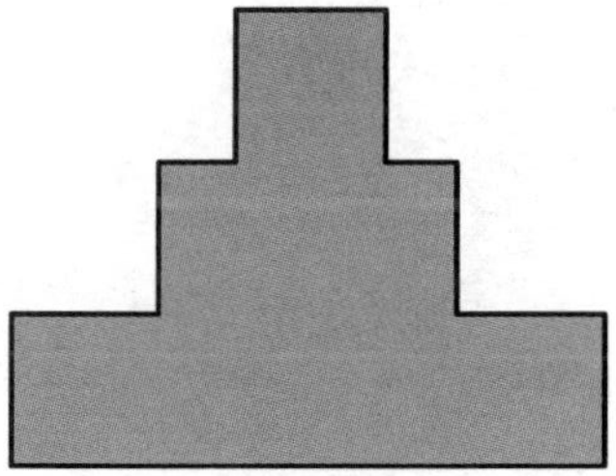

Area = ____ squares

Skill: Area

GUESS AGAIN

Use the clues to figure out what time it is.

- It is later than 3:59.
- The hour is an odd number.
- It is earlier than 7:00.
- It is just past the half hour.
- The first and last number of the time are the same.

What time is it?

☐ : ☐☐

- In 20 minutes, it will be the next hour.
- It is later than 12:00.
- It is earlier than 4:00.
- The hour is a number you might think of with twins or pairs.

What time is it?

☐ : ☐☐

Skill: Telling Time

- The two digits that make up the hour are the same.
- The minute hand is pointing to an odd number.
- It is later than 50 minutes past the hour.
- In 1 minute, the clock will strike the hour.

What time is it?

☐☐ : ☐☐

- The hour is an even number.
- It is earlier than 8:00.
- It is later than 5:00.
- The minutes can be evenly divided by 11.
- In 1 minute, it will be a quarter before the hour.

What time is it?

☐ : ☐☐

Magic Square

Look at the value for each animal. Then, add the rows and columns using the code. Write the sums in the blanks.

$= 150$

$= 60$

$= 4$

$= 45$

e(quation)
sen+sation

Some numbers in the equations have been replaced by letters. Each letter stands for the same number in all the equations. Figure out which letter represents each number and write it in the code.

1. $12 \times B = 6D$

2. $1D \times S = 90$

3. $X \times P = 32$

4. $B \times W = 30$

5. $11 \times M = M3$

6. $R \times C6 = 32$

7. $R5 \times 3 = 7B$

8. $R7 \times R = 5P$

9. $9 \times T = 6M$

10. $M2 \times 3 = 9W$

1 = ☐   2 = ☐   3 = ☐   4 = ☐   5 = ☐

6 = ☐   7 = ☐   8 = ☐   9 = ☐   0 = ☐

On the Lookout!

Hidden in the puzzle are 12 addition problems. One is circled for you. Can you find the rest? Use the boxes to write each equation you find.

Example / answer boxes:

$$4 + 5 = 9$$

	+	=
4	5	9
☐	☐	☐
☐	☐	☐
☐	☐	☐
☐	☐	☐
☐	☐	☐
☐	☐	☐
☐	☐	☐
☐	☐	☐
☐	☐	☐
☐	☐	☐
☐	☐	☐

Number-search puzzle grid (one equation, 4 + 5 = 9, is circled):

9	1	27	22	14	16	26	12	4	17	14	7	18	8	5	24
6	13	20	5	15	6	4	17	18	25	22	11	8	5	11	2
26	10	7	10	9	18	25	7	22	15	18	22	5	25	13	20
4	2	14	4	27	11	14	3	18	22	5	**(4**	16	9	17	22
5	14	4	6	14	6	14	3	5	**4**	**5**	**9)**	14	13	20	3
21	7	23	17	3	18	5	9	24	17	20	3	13	30	2	25
8	12	19	20	19	14	25	13	2	20	16	9	13	15	14	27
14	15	15	30	13	9	17	20	22	3	9	14	28	15	25	25
6	27	25	2	14	28	8	3	3	13	14	28	8	3	27	6

PATTERN POWER

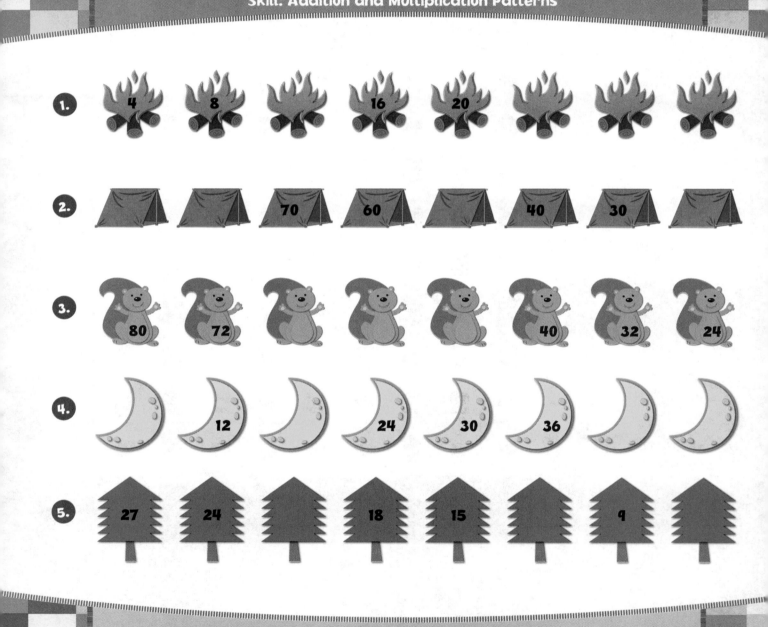

1. 4 8 ___ 16 20 ___ ___ ___

2. ___ ___ 70 60 ___ 40 30 ___

3. 80 72 ___ ___ ___ 40 32 24

4. ___ 12 ___ 24 30 36 ___ ___

5. 27 24 ___ ___ 18 15 ___ 9 ___

Write the missing numbers in each pattern.

The rocket is _____ inches long.

Then, use the ruler to measure the rocket to the nearest quarter inch. Write the measurement in the blank.

Cut out the rocket pieces and assemble them next to the ruler.

Skill: Measuring Length

NUMBER CROSS

Skills: Subtraction, Place Value

You are trapped inside a locked room. Only a secret code will unlock the door. Luckily, you can find the code by writing the numbers shown in the puzzle. All but two of the numbers will fit. The difference between the two leftover numbers is the code that sets you free.

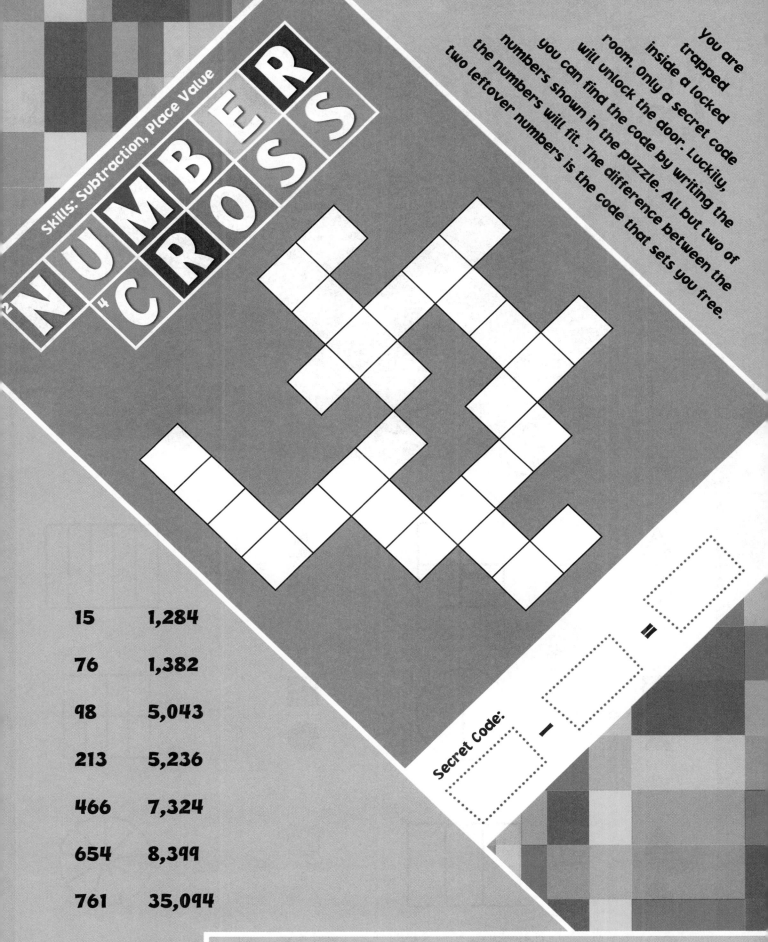

15	1,284
76	1,382
98	5,043
213	5,236
466	7,324
654	8,399
761	35,094

Secret Code: ☐ – ☐ ═ ☐

DARE TO DECODE

Use the key to decode the fractions. Then, color in the shapes to show each fraction.

CODE KEY

1	2	3	4	5	6	7	8	9
■	▲	▲	●	●	■	■	●	△

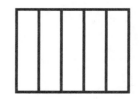

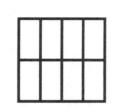

Each group of pictures shows a multiplication problem. Fill in the blanks to complete the problem. Draw your own picture to show the last problem.

⬜ × ⬜ = 12

⬜ × ⬜ = 40

⬜ × ⬜ = 14

⬜ × ⬜ = 45

3 × 6 = 18

Picture Perfect!

1. 12 × 4 =

2. 80 ÷ 5 =

3. 2 × 16 =

4. 63 ÷ 7 =

5. 45 ÷ 3 =

6. 6 × 11 =

7. 13 × 3 =

8. 72 ÷ 8 =

On THE DOT

Skills: Multiplication, Division

A well-known constellation is hidden in the stars below. Solve each equation. Connect the numbered stars in the order of your answers to reveal the constellation.

24 ★

67 ★

33 ★

17 ★   84 ★

53 ★

10 ★   99 ★

8 ★

16 ★   15 ★

48 ★   32 ★   9 ★

27 ★

14 ★

65 ★   21 ★

39 ★   66 ★

19 ★

44 ★

93 ★   73 ★   87 ★

Skill: Equivalent Fractions

Cut out the puzzle pieces. Put them together to discover a new friend. When the puzzle is solved correctly, equivalent fractions will be next to each other. There are four trios of equivalent fractions in the puzzle.

22	15	7	14	21	28	33	48
13	6	0	22	31	35	47	54
20	19	5	29	40	42	50	61
21	14	12	18	47	49	57	69
35	21	48	55	56	52	55	72
50	54	62	63	69	77	83	79
65	66	70	68	74	87	81	85
71	77	84	91	98	90	92	99

$$7 \times \square = \square$$

Seven is your lucky number for this puzzle. Start at 0. Keep adding 7 to find the correct path through the maze. When you cannot go any further following this pattern, you have reached the end. The last step is to write a multiplication problem to describe the final square in the path.

Math path

GUESS AGAIN

Use each set of clues to discover the mystery number.

Start with the quotient of 48 ÷ 4.

Add 9.

Divide the new number by 7.

Add 15.

The mystery number is

Start with the number of feet in 2 yards.

Multiply the number by 4.

Switch the digits' places.

Divide the new number by 7.

The mystery number is

Skills: Multiplication, Division

It is a two-digit number.

Both digits are odd numbers.

Added together, the digits equal 3 × 4.

The second digit minus the first digit equals 2.

The mystery number is

It is a two-digit number.

The product of the digits is 12.

The larger digit divided by the smaller equals 3.

The smaller digit comes first.

The mystery number is

MASTER SHAPE

Use a ruler to divide the picture into $\frac{1}{2}$-inch squares. Count the squares you used and write the number in the blank.

Area = ☐ $\frac{1}{2}$-inch squares

Skills: Area, Measuring Length

PATTERN POWER

| 64 | | 48 | 40 | 32 | | 16 |

| 14 | 28 | | 56 | 70 | | 98 |

| 10 | 12 | 16 | | 30 | 40 | |

| 85 | 80 | 70 | 65 | 55 | | |

| 18 | | 36 | 45 | | 63 | |

Write the missing numbers in each pattern.

STORY STUMPERS

Skill: Quadrilaterals

Paintings in Mrs. Bentangle's house are displayed in unusual frames. Read the clues to discover which painting belongs in which frame. Then, draw each picture in its correct frame.

- The frame for the painting of a horse is a quadrilateral with four equal sides and four equal angles.

- The frame for the painting of the ocean is a quadrilateral with no equal angles.

- The frame for the painting of a woman's face is a not a quadrilateral.

- The frame for the painting of an interesting pattern is a quadrilateral with two sets of parallel sides.

- The frame for the painting of a race car is a quadrilateral with one set of parallel sides.

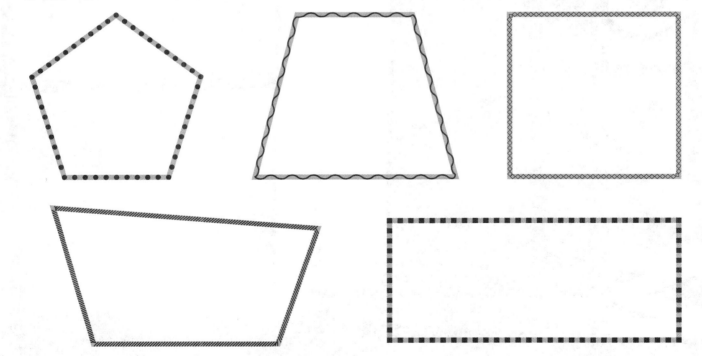

Magic Square

The numbers shown by the dice in each row and column follow a pattern. Figure out the pattern. Then, draw the missing dice. Finally, finish the sentence below.

The pattern is: _____

The distance from one dot to the next equals one unit. Can you use the dots to draw a shape that has a perimeter of exactly 55? It can be any shape you want, but it must be a closed shape. You might want to use a pencil for easy erasing!

DRAW

Skill: Perimeter

e(quation) / sen+sation

Skills: Addition, Subtraction

Someone has stolen the numbers from these equations. Use logic and your knowledge of operations to replace the missing numbers.

$$\begin{array}{r} 4\ \ 2\ \ \square \\ +\ \ \square\ \ \square\ \ 7 \\ \hline 6\ \ 1\ \ 9 \end{array}$$

$$\begin{array}{r} \square\ \ 8\ \ \square \\ -\ \ 5\ \ 9\ \ 3 \\ \hline 3\ \ \square\ \ 4 \end{array}$$

$$\begin{array}{r} \square\ \ \square\ \ 9 \\ +\ \ \square\ \ 2\ \ \square \\ \hline 3\ \ 1\ \ 8 \end{array}$$

$$\begin{array}{r} \square\ \ \square\ \ 2 \\ -\ \ \square\ \ 8\ \ \square \\ \hline 8\ \ 5 \end{array}$$

Are you ready to set sail for the land of equivalent fractions? Draw a line to connect each pair of equivalent fractions in the puzzle. Then, color in all the enclosed sections to reveal the vehicle for your travels.

On THE DOT

Skill: Equivalent Fractions

$\frac{4}{6}$

$\frac{1}{2}$ $\frac{1}{8}$

$\frac{1}{4}$ $\frac{3}{9}$ $\frac{1}{3}$ $\frac{2}{7}$

$\frac{3}{6}$

$\frac{3}{5}$ $\frac{2}{16}$ $\frac{2}{3}$ $\frac{6}{10}$

$\frac{1}{6}$ $\frac{2}{12}$

$\frac{2}{8}$ $\frac{4}{14}$

NUMBER CROSS

Across

2. 5 + 5 + 5 + 5 + 5 + 5
6. 2 + 2 + 2
8. 2 + 2 + 2 + 2 + 2
9. 18 + 18
10. 4 + 4 + 4
13. 12
14. 10 + 10
15. 8 + 8 + 8 + 8 + 8 + 8
16. 30 + 30

$$5 \times 6 = 30$$

Read each addition pattern. Then, write the related multiplication equation in the puzzle. One is done for you.

Down

1. 1 + 1
2. 5 + 5
3. 6 + 6 + 6
4. 9 + 9 + 9 + 9
5. 3 + 3 + 3 + 3 + 3
7. 6 + 6
10. 4 + 4 + 4 + 4 + 4 + 4 + 4 + 4 + 4 + 4 + 4 + 4
11. 3 + 3 + 3 + 3 + 3 + 3 + 3 + 3 + 3 + 3
12. 3 + 3 + 3 + 3 + 3 + 3 + 3 + 3 + 3 + 3 + 3 + 3 + 3 + 3 + 3 + 3 + 3 + 3 + 3 + 3

DARE TO DECODE

Each colored shape represents a different fraction. Use the clues comparing the fractions to crack the code. Draw the colored shapes to complete the key.

CODE KEY

$\frac{1}{4}$	$\frac{1}{2}$	$\frac{1}{3}$	$\frac{3}{6}$	$\frac{2}{8}$	$\frac{1}{10}$

A Show of Hands

Skills: Measuring Volume,
Measuring Mass

Cut out the pictures. Decide
which metric unit would best
measure the item: liters, grams,
or kilograms. Glue or tape each
picture in the correct column.

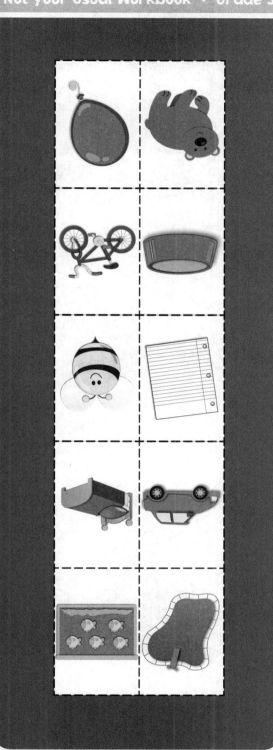

grams	kilograms	liters

Skill: Multiples of 10

Cut out the pieces. Match the multiplication equations with the products.

Round each number to the nearest 10. Circle your choice. Then, use the number choices that are left over to unlock a secret message.

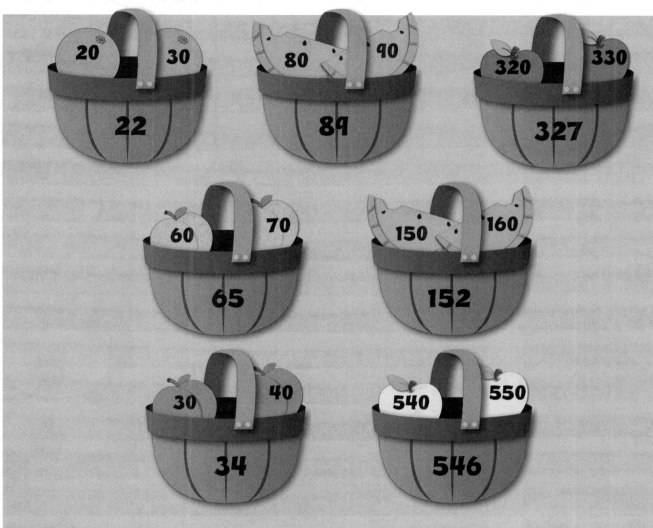

Code:

30 = don't   40 = or   60 = round   80 = forget   160 = up   320 = to   540 = down

Secret message:

_____ _____ _____ _____ _____ _____ _____ !

Picture Perfect!

24 ÷ 6 = 4

1	5	11	35	6	21	9	8
95	20	100	50	36	7	16	5
80	42	60	10	22	3	1	25
8	45	3	5	20	80	24	66
10	8	4	68	9	3	3	42
4	32	24	2	12	50	72	6
11	60	16	32	48	36	52	7
81	9	9	21	12	2	6	68

20 18 76 12 40

Skill: Division

Find and circle 10 division problems in the puzzle. Complete each problem you circle by writing a division sign (÷) and an equal sign (=). One is done for you.

PATTERN POWER

1.

2.

3.

4.

Draw the missing hands on the blank clocks to finish each pattern.

$\frac{1}{6}$	$\frac{1}{10}$	$\frac{1}{8}$	$\frac{1}{16}$	$\frac{5}{6}$	$\frac{3}{3}$	$\frac{3}{4}$	$\frac{7}{8}$
$\frac{1}{7}$	$\frac{1}{5}$	$\frac{1}{4}$	$\frac{1}{3}$	$\frac{2}{2}$	$\frac{2}{3}$	$\frac{11}{12}$	$\frac{1}{1}$
$\frac{1}{8}$	$\frac{1}{9}$	$\frac{2}{12}$	$\frac{1}{2}$	$\frac{1}{2}$	$\frac{7}{8}$	$\frac{4}{5}$	$\frac{1}{3}$
$\frac{6}{6}$	$\frac{4}{5}$	$\frac{2}{3}$	$\frac{2}{5}$	$\frac{5}{8}$	$\frac{3}{8}$	$\frac{1}{4}$	$\frac{1}{8}$

To find a path through the maze on the left, start at $\frac{1}{6}$. Then, move to a space that has a larger fraction. To find a path through the maze on the right, start at $\frac{7}{8}$. Then, move to a space that has a smaller fraction. Circle the last fraction in each path.

Math 4 path

GUESS AGAIN

Use each set of clues to discover the mystery number.

- Start with the number of sides on an octagon.
- Multiply by the number of sides on a triangle.
- Divide by the number of sides on a hexagon.
- To the quotient, add the number of sides on a pentagon.

The mystery number is ____.

- The mystery number has three different digits.
- The sum of all three digits is 3.
- The mystery number is greater than 100.
- The mystery number is less than 115.

The mystery number is ____.

Skills: Multiplication, Division

- Start with the number of quarters in one dollar.
- Multiply by the number of dimes in one dollar.
- Divide by the number of nickels in one dollar.
- Add the number of pennies in one quarter.

The mystery number is ____.

- The mystery number has two digits.
- The first digit is greater than the second digit.
- The sum of the digits is 7, and the difference is 1.
- The mystery number is less than 50.

The mystery number is ____.

Magic Square

Place or draw coins on the empty squares so that each row, column, and diagonal adds to the same amount of money. Write the amount in the blank below.

Each row, column, and diagonal has [   ] ¢.

10¢ 1¢
1¢ 1¢

1¢ 1¢
1¢

10¢ 5¢
1¢

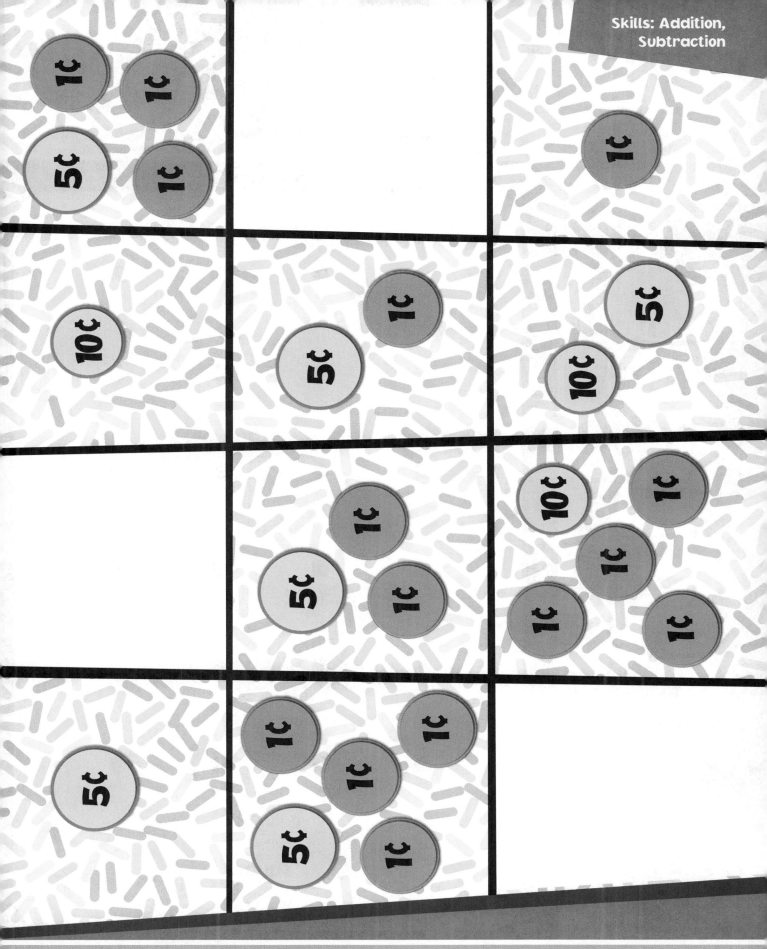

Use the dots to draw squares. They can be any size, and the squares can overlap. How many total squares can you draw? Write the number in the blank.

DRAW

QUICK

Skill: Quadrilaterals

I drew _____ squares.

e(quation) sen+sation

Skills: Addition, Subtraction, Multiplication, Division

Each equation includes the numbers 1 through 9. Each number appears just once in each equation before the equal sign. Do the operations from left to right. Fill in the missing numbers. One is done for you.

1. $2 + \boxed{6} \times 1 - \boxed{4} \times 3 + \boxed{9} \div 7 + \boxed{8} \times 5 = 55$

2. $9 + \boxed{} - 6 \times \boxed{} - 4 + \boxed{} + 8 \div \boxed{} - 2 = 3$

3. $1 + \boxed{} \div 2 + \boxed{} \times 7 \div \boxed{} + 4 - \boxed{} + 6 = 12$

4. $4 \times \boxed{} + 6 - \boxed{} \div 9 \times \boxed{} + 1 + \boxed{} \div 3 = 4$

5. $8 - \boxed{} \times 5 \times \boxed{} - 6 \div \boxed{} + 7 - \boxed{} \div 1 = 9$

STORY STUMPERS

Students in room 217 voted on their favorite sports. The results are shown in the bar graph. But someone forgot to label the graph! Read the clues and write a label for each bar in the graph.

Skill: Bar Graphs

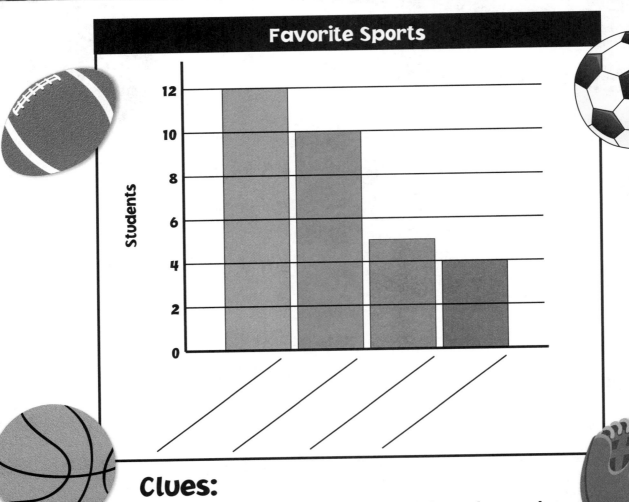

Favorite Sports

Students

12
10
8
6
4
2
0

Clues:
Soccer is neither the most nor the least popular sport.
Football received more votes than baseball.
Basketball is either the most or the least popular sport.
Football received fewer votes than soccer.

MASTER SHAPE

Cut out the shapes and assemble them into a rectangle. The sides of the shapes are labeled with their lengths in units. Use the measurements to find the total area of the rectangle and write it in the blank.

Area = [   ] square units

Skill: Area

NUMBER CROSS

Skills: Multiplication, Division

Across

2. 5 × 5 and 7 × 7
6. 10 × 10 and 60 ÷ 15
7. 5 × 6 and 32 ÷ 2
9. 42 ÷ 7 and 2 × 11
10. 9 × 11 and 13 × 4
12. 81 ÷ 9 and 28 ÷ 7
13. 8 × 7 and 24 × 2

Across, continued

14. 80 ÷ 20 and 38 ÷ 19
16. 63 ÷ 9 and 100 ÷ 10
17. 15 × 3 and 10 × 5

Down

1. 8 × 2 and 56 ÷ 2
2. 4 × 11 and 8 × 4
3. 70 ÷ 7 and 3 × 3
4. 20 × 4 and 9 × 8
5. 13 × 3 and 12 × 7
8. 54 ÷ 3 and 31 × 2
10. 75 ÷ 15 and 24 ÷ 6
11. 30 × 3 and 80 ÷ 2
12. 7 × 2 and 12 × 8
15. 72 ÷ 12 and 9 × 3

Solve each pair of equations. Then, write both answers in the puzzle. You will need to decide which answer comes first. Two pairs are done for you.

A secret letter is hidden in the dots. Start at the number 3 and connect the dots counting by threes. When you reach the last possible number, draw a line back to where you began. Finally, use a ruler to measure the perimeter of the letter you found to the nearest centimeter. Fill in the blanks below.

Secret Letter:

Perimeter: _____ centimeters

On THE DOT

Skills: Perimeter, Measuring Length

• 43

12   • 26

9 •

• 67

4   • 20   91 •

8   18 •   • 15

1   2 •

17   21 •   • 24

6 •

82 •   13 •

22

30 •   • 27

19   44 •

3 •   • 55

71 •

52

• 29

3 •   • 33   38   34 •

A Show of Hands

Skill: Understanding Fractions

Cut out the fraction circles. Glue or tape each one next to the number line where it belongs. Write a fraction next to each piece.

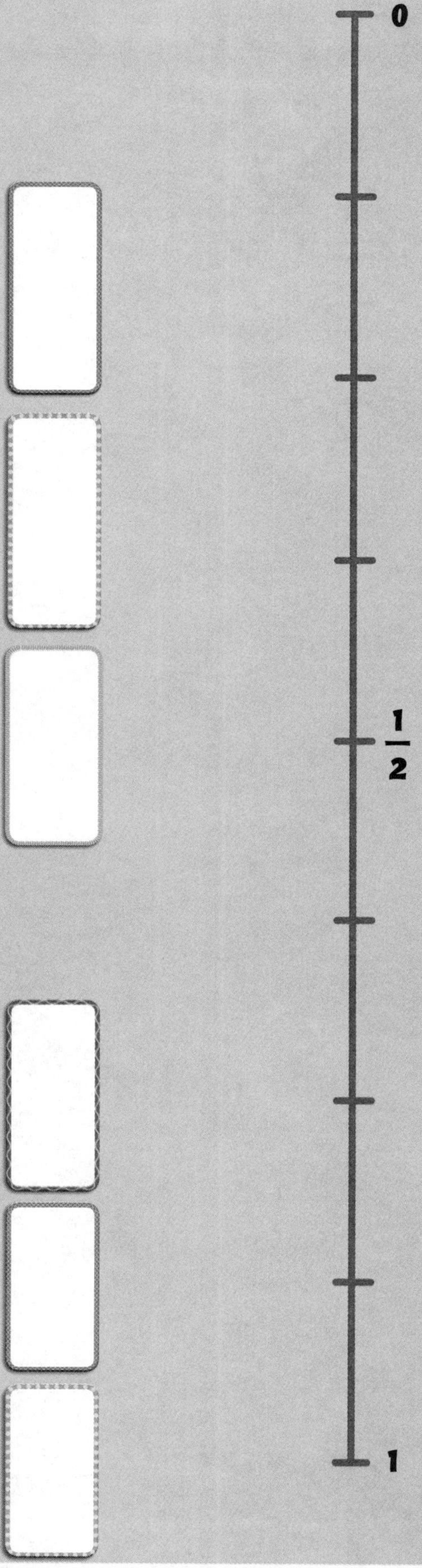

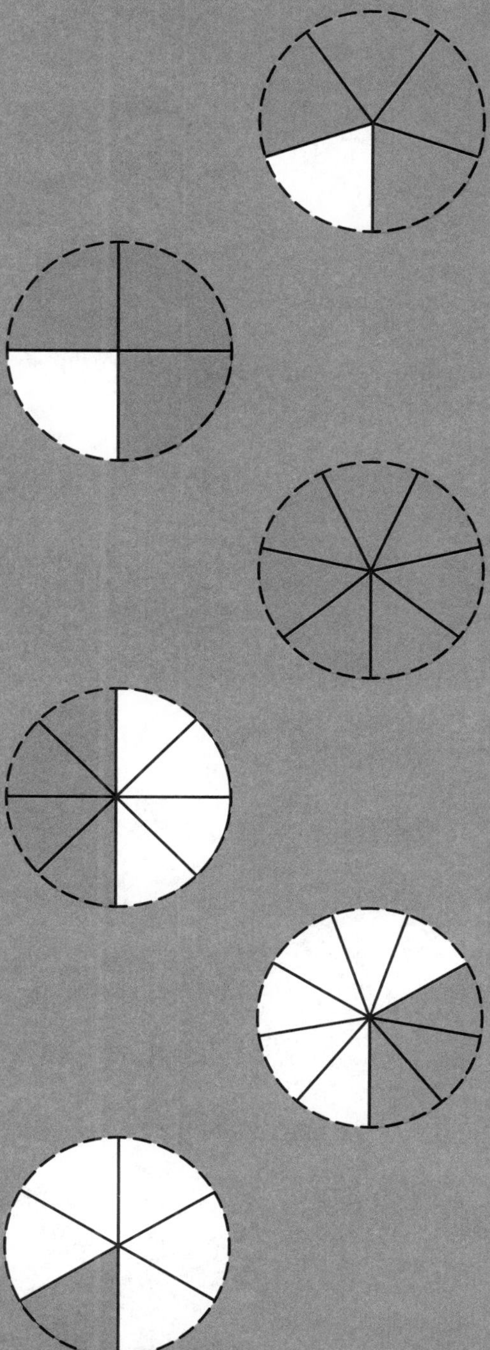

1

$\frac{1}{2}$

0

DARE TO DECODE

Skill: Multiplication

The equations and products below are written in code. Each number shown stands for a different number. Use what you know about multiplication to crack the code. One number is given for you. Hint: Each equation shows a number being multiplied by itself.

CODE KEY

Number in Code	1	2	3	4	5	6	7	8	9
Actual Number					8				

$5 \times 5 = 49$

$7 \times 7 = 7$

$8 \times 8 = 38$

$4 \times 4 = 24$

$3 \times 3 = 9$

$9 \times 9 = 74$

$2 \times 2 = 6$

$6 \times 6 = 57$

$1 \times 1 = 96$

It must be spring! It is time to plant the garden. Divide the garden into areas for each type of plant. Use the list of plants and the area that each plant needs.

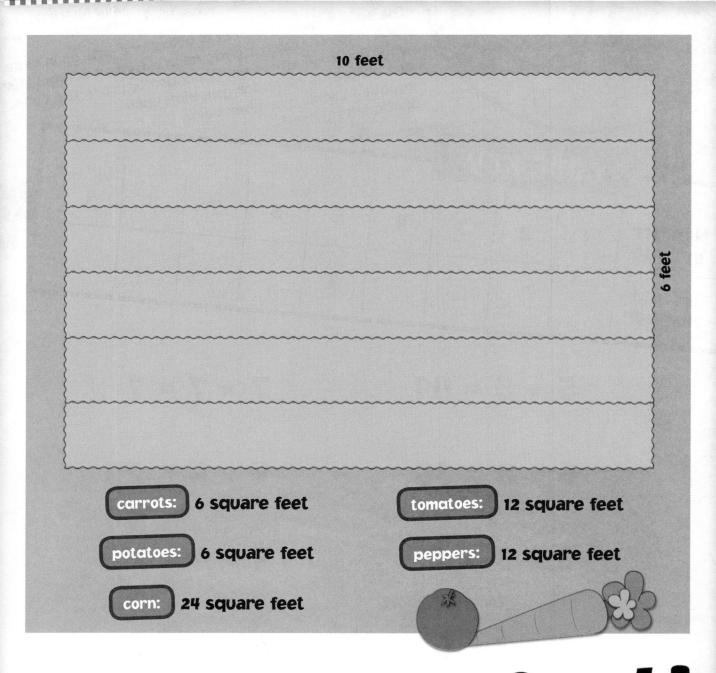

10 feet

6 feet

carrots:	6 square feet	tomatoes:	12 square feet
potatoes:	6 square feet	peppers:	12 square feet
corn:	24 square feet		

Picture Perfect!

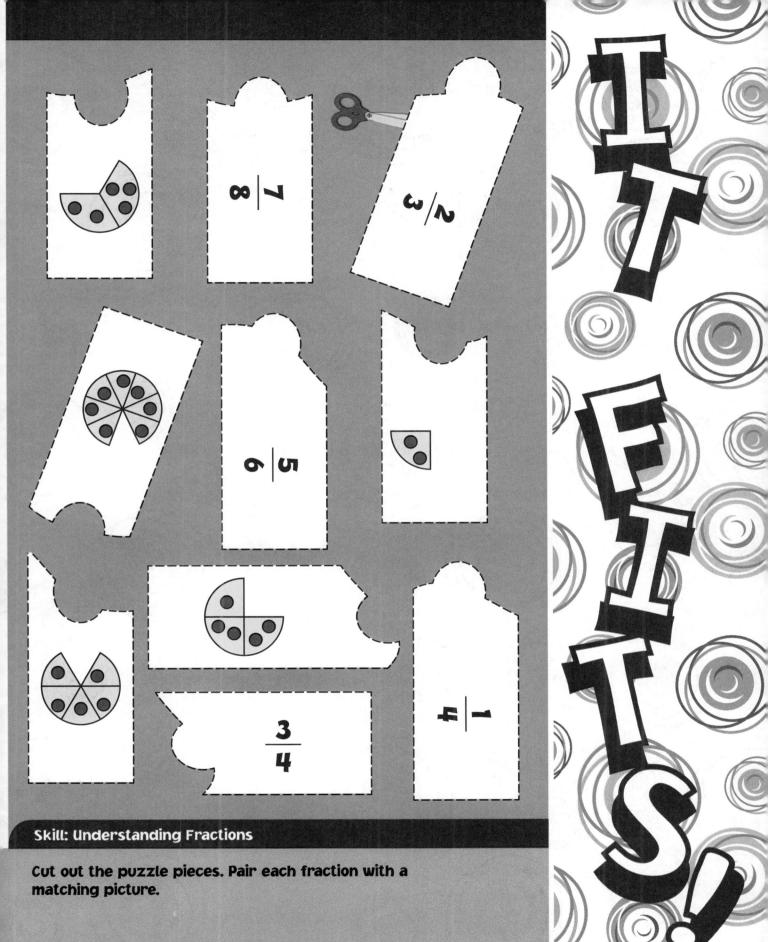

Cut out the puzzle pieces. Pair each fraction with a matching picture.

PATTERN POWER

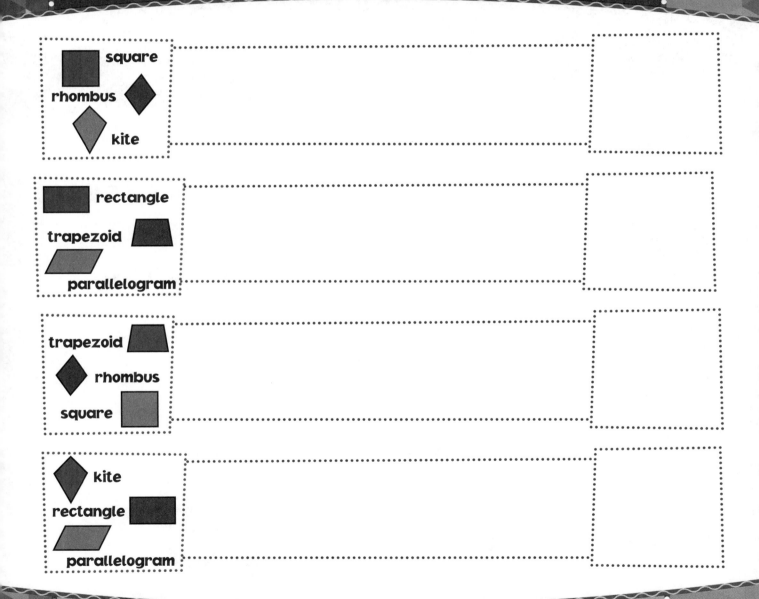

square	rhombus	kite
rectangle	trapezoid	parallelogram
trapezoid	rhombus	square
kite	rectangle	parallelogram

In each row, draw your own pattern using the quadrilaterals shown. Then, challenge a friend to continue your pattern by drawing the next shape in the blank box.

e(quation) sen+sation

These equations are missing their signs. Write +, −, ×, or ÷ on each star to make the equations true.

1. 16 ☆ 2 ☆ 5 = 3

2. 2 ☆ 3 ☆ 5 = 30

3. 15 ☆ 15 ☆ 3 = 10

4. 9 ☆ 9 ☆ 10 ☆ 4 = 75

5. 4 ☆ 6 ☆ 2 = 12

6. 50 ☆ 30 ☆ 6 = 120

7. 36 ☆ 6 ☆ 3 = 18

8. 8 ☆ 8 ☆ 6 = 70

1. 321 [ ]
2. 586 [ ]
3. 9,455 [ ]
4. 73 [ ]
5. 804 [ ]
6. 1,216 [ ]
7. 467 [ ]
8. 189 [ ]
9. 419 [ ]
10. 4,651 [ ]

ON THE DOT

Skill: Rounding

Round each number to the nearest 100. Connect the dots in the order of your answers.

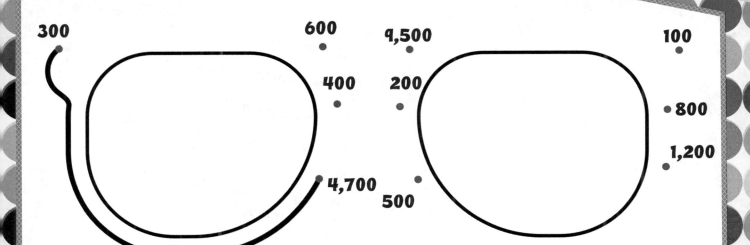

300   600   9,500   100
       400   200   800
                       1,200
       4,700 500

GUESS AGAIN

Use the clues to identify the fraction.
Circle your answer.

- My denominator is an even number.
- I am larger than $\frac{1}{2}$.
- My numerator is 3.
- I am equal to $\frac{6}{8}$.

$\frac{3}{6}$ $\frac{3}{4}$ $\frac{1}{3}$

- My numerator is 1 less than my denominator.
- I am greater than $\frac{1}{3}$.
- I could describe 2 siblings in a family of 3.
- I am equal to $\frac{4}{6}$.

$\frac{2}{3}$ $\frac{8}{12}$ $\frac{1}{2}$

Skills: Understanding Fractions, Equivalent Fractions

- My denominator is $\frac{1}{10}$ of 100.
- I am in my smallest form.
- My numerator is an odd number.
- My denominator is 1 more than my numerator.

$\frac{8}{9}$ $\frac{3}{10}$ $\frac{9}{10}$

- I am larger than $\frac{1}{4}$.
- I am smaller than $\frac{2}{3}$.
- I am probably the first fraction you learned.
- If I were money, I'd be equal to 2 quarters.

$\frac{1}{6}$ $\frac{1}{2}$ $\frac{4}{5}$

Multiply the number in the caterpillar's head by each number shown. Write your answers in the circles.

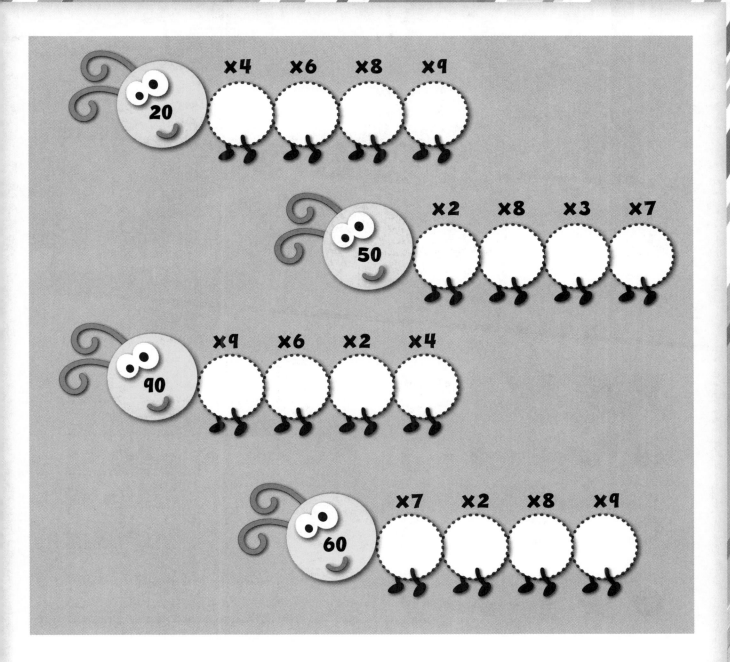

Picture Perfect!

DARE TO DECODE

Decide what digit each picture stands for. Complete the code. One digit is given for you. Write the division problems in the blanks. Hint: Use what you know about numbers multiplied by themselves.

CODE KEY

								9
Digit								

1. 🛸 🪐 ÷ 🪐 = 🪐   ☐ ÷ ☐ = ☐

2. 🛸 🌙 ÷ 🪐 = 🌙   ☐ ÷ ☐ = ☐

3. 🪐 👽 ÷ 🌙 = 🌙   ☐ ÷ ☐ = ☐

4. ⭐ 👽 ÷ 🛸 = 🌙   ☐ ÷ ☐ = ☐

5. ⭐ 🚀 ÷ 🛸 = ☄   ☐ ÷ ☐ = ☐

6. 🌙 🛸 ÷ ☄ = ☄   ☐ ÷ ☐ = ☐

STORY STUMPERS

1. A shelf holds 36 school supplies. A third are pencils. There are half as many erasers as pencils. There are 3 times as many bottles of glue as erasers. How many of each type of school supply are on the shelf?

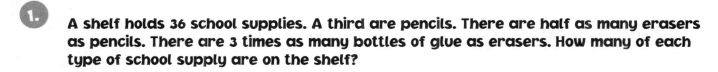

2. The Awesome Auto Sales car lot is full. 8 of the cars are blue. There are half as many yellow cars as blue cars. There are twice as many white cars as blue and yellow cars. There are 10 fewer gray cars than white cars. How many cars can the car lot hold?

[   ] cars

3. The Cat Cottage animal shelter has 27 cats. Less than half of the cats are white. There are $\frac{1}{6}$ as many black cats as white ones. There are $\frac{1}{2}$ as many orange cats as white ones. There are twice as many brown cats as black. There are $\frac{1}{4}$ as many gray cats as white. How many of each kind of cat does the shelter have?

$$10 \times 3 = 30$$

			2	4	7	28
11	1	45	9	72	15	12
32	18	6	6	36	9	4
5	32	7	25	4	2	16
3	6	9	24	1	18	7
15	8	5	40	5	20	8
20	3	6	81	6	8	48

Skill: Multiplication

Find and circle 7 multiplication problems hidden in the puzzle. Add multiplication and equal symbols to complete the problems you find. One is done for you.

Not Your Usual Workbook · Grade 3

Fill in the bar graph to show what Connor collected at the beach.

Found at the Beach

Picture Perfect!

Magic Square

The numbers shown by the cards in each row and column follow the same pattern to produce a final number. One number has been provided for you. Follow the pattern to write numbers in the other spaces. Finally, finish the sentence below.

The pattern is: _____

40

Skill: Telling Time
NUMBER CROSS

1. **5.**

6. **9.**

10.

Down

2. **3.**

4. **7.** **8.**

Read the time on each clock. Write the time in the puzzle, but do not include the colon. One is done for you.

Cut out the triangles. Use them to make these quadrilaterals:

- rectangle
- square
- rhombus
- trapezoid
- kite

MASTER SHAPE

The distance from one dot to the next equals one unit. Can you use the dots to draw a shape that has an area of exactly 175 square units? It can be any shape you want, but it must be a closed shape. You might want to use a pencil for easy erasing!

DRAW

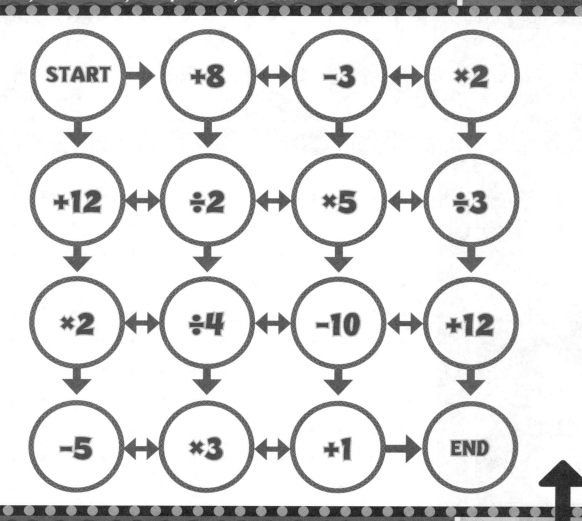

Start with 0. Find a path through the maze so that you end up with 16. Follow the arrows and perform each operation. Keep a running total as you go. There is only one correct path.

Math path

PATTERN POWER

1. $\dfrac{3}{4}$ ⬚ $\dfrac{9}{12}$ $\dfrac{12}{16}$ ◯

2. ⬚ $\dfrac{2}{4}$ $\dfrac{3}{6}$ $\dfrac{4}{8}$ ◯

3. $\dfrac{1}{3}$ ⬚ $\dfrac{9}{27}$ $\dfrac{27}{81}$ ◯

4. $\dfrac{1}{4}$ ⬚ $\dfrac{4}{16}$ $\dfrac{8}{32}$ ◯

5. ⬚ $\dfrac{4}{6}$ $\dfrac{6}{9}$ $\dfrac{8}{12}$ ◯

Write the missing equivalent fraction in each pattern. Then, divide and color the circle to show the fraction you wrote.

e(quation) sen+sation

Someone has stolen the numbers from these equations. Use logic and your knowledge of mathematics to replace the missing numbers.

$$
\begin{array}{r}
5\;\;2\;\;15 \\
-\;\;2\;\;4\;\;8 \\
\hline
3\;\;8\;\;7
\end{array}
$$

$$
\begin{array}{r}
\square\;\;\square\;\;8 \\
+\;\;2\;\;2\;\;\square \\
\hline
6\;\;7\;\;0
\end{array}
$$

$$
\begin{array}{r}
5\;\;\square\;\;\square \\
-\;\;\square\;\;8\;\;9 \\
\hline
2\;\;1\;\;9
\end{array}
$$

$$
\begin{array}{r}
1\;\;4\;\;\square \\
+\;\;\square\;\;5\;\;8 \\
\hline
5\;\;\square\;\;4
\end{array}
$$

A Show of Hands

Equation #1

Equation #2

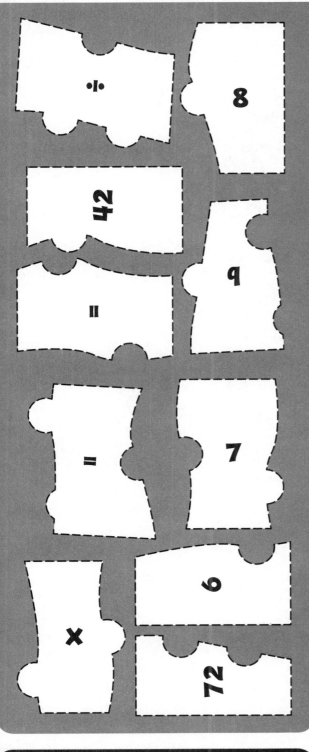

Pieces shown (as numbers and symbols):

- ÷
- 8
- 42
- 9
- =
- =
- 7
- 6
- ×
- 72

Cut out the puzzle pieces. Put them together to make two equations. Tape or glue the equations in the space shown.

Skills: Multiplication, Division

GUESS AGAIN

Use each set of clues to discover
the mystery number.

If you add 20, the sum is greater than 100.

If you subtract 20, the difference is less than 65.

It can be divided evenly by 7.

It is an even number.

The mystery number is

Start with the quotient of 51 ÷ 3.

Add 1.

Switch the digits' places.

Divide the new number by 9.

The mystery number is

Skills: Multiplication, Division, Place Value

It has 2 digits.

The first digit is 3 times the second digit.

The difference between the 2 digits is 6.

The mystery number is

It has 2 digits.

The second digit is half the first digit.

The sum of the two digits is 9.

The mystery number is

DARE TO DECODE

Decode the fractions on the number lines. Write numbers to complete the code.

CODE KEY

Number						

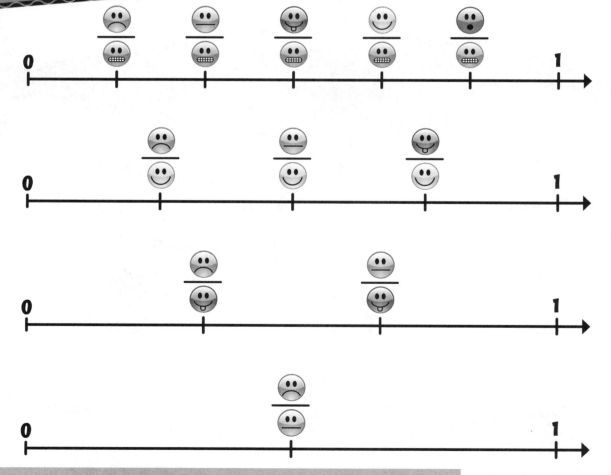

LANGUAGE ARTS

Read each clue. Write a matching word in the boxes. Cross out letters inside the teddy bear as you use them. The letters that are left over will spell a secret adjective that means "nice to look at."

Traveling on a gravel road

The opposite of short

The color of a teddy bear

Having lots of muscles

Like a racehorse

Secret Adjective:

t n m p b
r s f b r o e
t a t w s n p
u r l y o n t
g o y g

Skill: Using Commas

Begin at START. Follow the arrows to find words that make up a secret sentence. Write the sentence on the lines, capitalizing letters where needed. Also add the correct punctuation to your sentence, including commas.

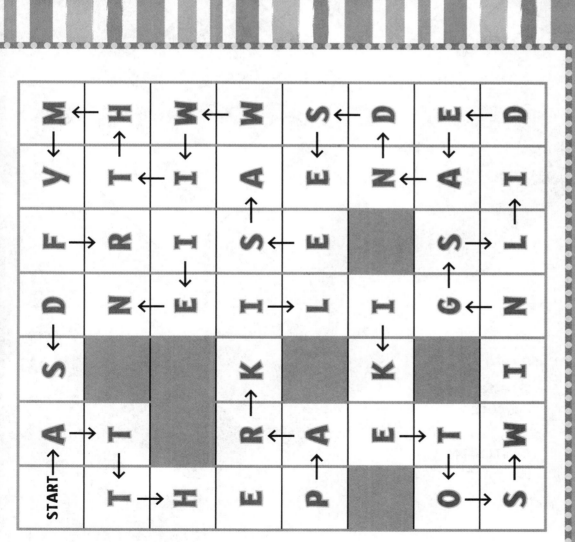

GO ON ACROSS

Abstract nouns do not name people, places, or objects. Instead, they name ideas and feelings. Fit the abstract nouns into the puzzle.

3-Letter Words:
joy
law

4-Letter Words:
love
luck

5-Letter Words:
honor
power

6-Letter Words:
relief
talent

7-Letter Word:
courage

8-Letter Word:
laughter

Sudoku for you

Skills: Spelling, Plurals

Write letters in the spaces so that each row and column contains the letters to spell the plural of "box." No letter should appear twice in the same row or column. Do not guess. Use logic!

	E	O		
B				
			S	
				X

Because it snowed all night,

so he was grumpy all day.

Carmen lost her wallet,

because he is allergic to them.

so my dog began to bark.

Micah didn't sleep well,

there was no school today.

Austin can't eat peanuts

and now she has no money.

Someone knocked at the door,

Draw a line to match each cloud to an umbrella to show cause and effect.

MIRROR MIRROR

1. unkind or cruel

   harsh _____

2. to travel around an unknown place

   explore _____

3. flat land with no trees where the ground is always frozen

   tundra _____

4. to travel from one area to another at different times of year

   migrate _____

5. weather in an area over a long period of time

   climate _____

6. relating to the area around the North Pole

   Arctic _____

Read each definition. Hold the page up to a mirror to read the matching word. Write the word on the line. Make sure it is facing the right direction!

Read each word root. On the sunrays, write words that contain the root.

symphony   microphone   phonics   kaleidoscope

microscope   stethoscope   phonograph   telescope

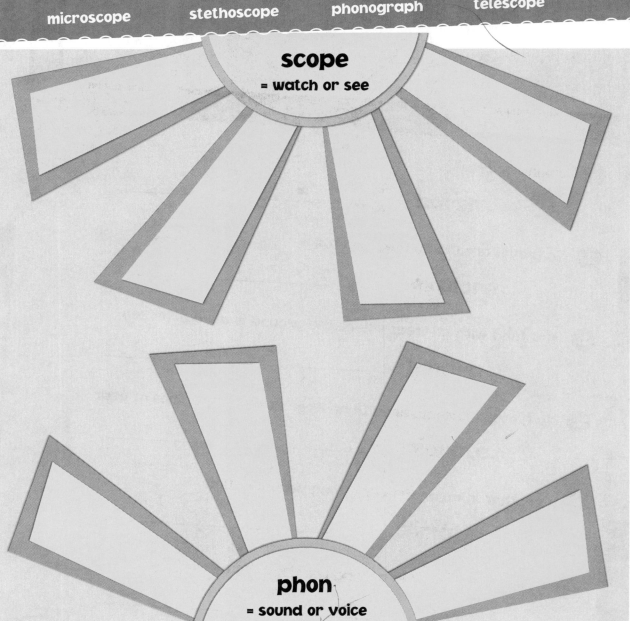

scope
= watch or see

phon
= sound or voice

Picture This!

Brainstorm an action verb that begins with each letter of the alphabet. Some are provided for you.

Skill: Verbs

Action Verbs

A   action
B   **bounce**
C   call
D   do
E   eat
F   **flip**
G   go
H   hide
I   illustrate
J   jump
K   kick
L   **lick**
M   mumble

N   nudge
O   open
P   pop
Q   quick
R   **run**
S   swirl
T   **twirl**
U   use
V   vibrat
W   **wink**
X   yo-yo
Y
Z   zoom

ALPHA-
CHALLENGE

RIDDLE ME

Write the adjective that completes each hink pink.

Skill: Adjectives

A hink pink is a pair of rhyming words that answer a riddle.

Examples: smart heart, spring king

1. What is a rabbit with a sense of humor? a _____ bunny

5. What is a lengthy tune? a _____ song

8. What is another name for a large truck? a _____ rig

2. What is an empty seat? a _____ chair

6. What is an annoying insect that isn't wet? a _____ fly

3. What would you call a chubby kitty? a _____ cat

7. What is a father who feels unhappy? a _____ dad

4. What is another name for a tight carpet? a _____ rug

#4

#3

#2

#1

It's time for Top Five! Write five sentences describing your top five favorite summer activities. Each sentence should contain a conjunction from the box. Use each word only once. You will not use all the conjunctions.

Word Box

next	after	or
and	if	but
so	because	before

Skill: Using Conjunctions

QUIZ WHIZ

Skill: Subject-Verb Agreement

Sentence Scramble

Draw a line to connect the words and form a sentence. Skip one verb that does not agree with the subject of the sentence. Write the sentence at the bottom of the page.

The

blooming

are

garden

flowers

my

is

in

brightly.

PREST-O CHANGE-O!

Skill: Parts of Speech

How do you make mice jump? By changing one letter at a time! Write a word for each clue. Each word should be the same as the word above it except for one changed letter. The clues are action verbs. The words you write will be nouns related to the actions.

roll

spend

squeeze

bend

bleat

brighten

swell

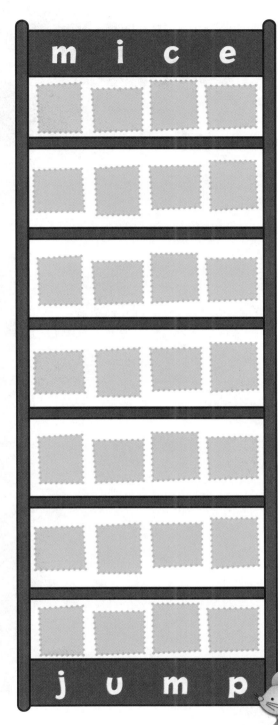

m i c e

j u m p

WORD MATH

Skill: Capitalizing Titles

Each rebus leads to a word in the title of a popular book. Write each title on the lines. Be sure to capitalize all important words in each title.

1.  — w + i + 🌀 − f

2. 👧 − gr + 📓

3. ☕ − f

Book Title:

The _____ _____

the _____

Book Title:

_____ _____

and the

_____ of

_____

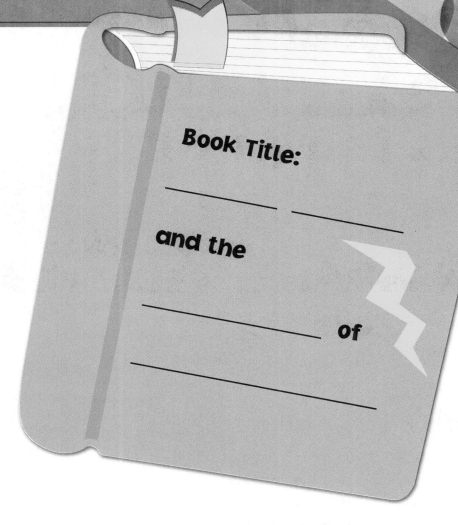

1. 🎩 − t + 🍒 − che

2. 🍳 + ⛺ − nt + r

3. 🪑 − ir + m + 🐻 − a

4. 7 − ven + cr + 🥅 🥅 − n

In Search Of

Skill: Interjections

Yay!
Find these
interjections:

hooray
yahoo
yippee
hallelujah
achoo
darn
phew
yikes
ouch
whoops
holy cow
gosh

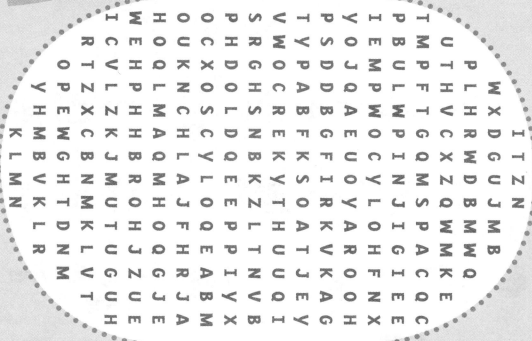

CODE BREAKER

Skills: Context Clues, Idioms, Spelling

A well-known saying appears below written in code. Can you crack the code? Use the hints. Keep track of each letter using the chart.

Rmzhapd dtcrf nawlcx zbrp saxld.

__ __ __ __ __ __ __

__ __ __ __ __

__ __ __ __ __ __ __ __ __ __

__ __ __ __ __ .

Hints:

I always **dzxczmb** before I exercise.

___ ___ ___ ___ ___ ___ ___

A **vcoxr'd** stripes help it hide from predators.

___ ___ ___ ___ ___ ' ___

Mr. Harrison grilled **breowxycxd** for the scouts.

___ ___ ___ ___ ___ ___ ___ ___ ___ ___

Jules Verne wrote Around the **Saxnl** in Eighty Days.

___ ___ ___ ___ ___

Code Chart

A	B	C	D	E	F	G	H	I	J	K	L	M

N	O	P	Q	R	S	T	U	V	W	X	Y	Z

GO ON ACROSS

Skills: Vocabulary, Spelling

The answer to each clue is a four-letter word. Write the words in the puzzle, starting from the outer squares and working in. Then, read clockwise around the gray squares, starting at number 9, to find the secret word.

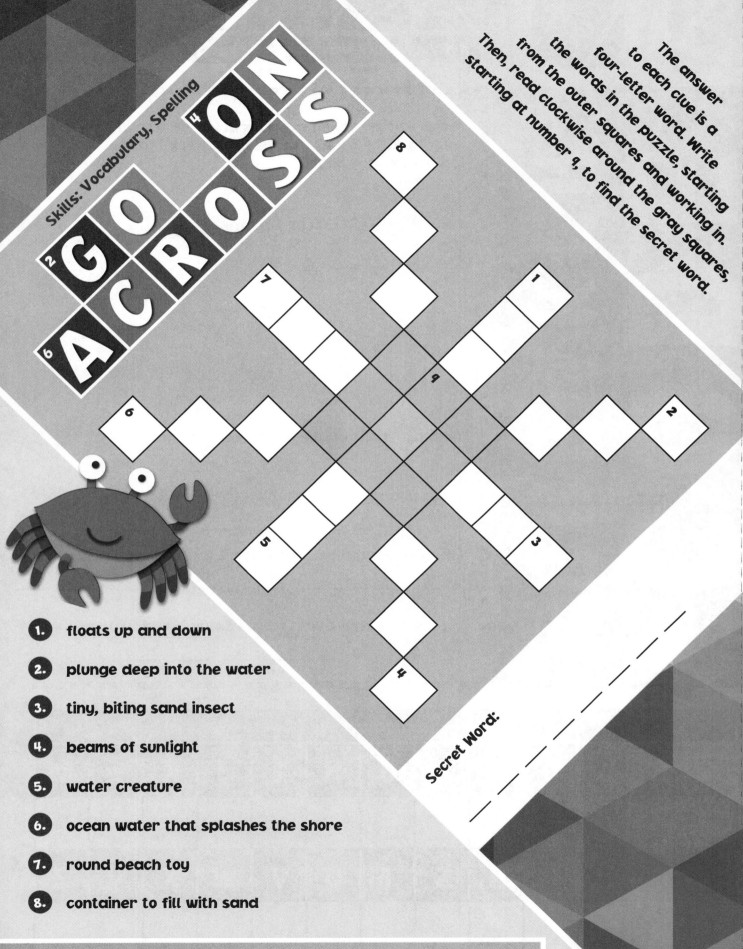

Secret Word: _ _ _ _

1. floats up and down

2. plunge deep into the water

3. tiny, biting sand insect

4. beams of sunlight

5. water creature

6. ocean water that splashes the shore

7. round beach toy

8. container to fill with sand

JUMBLED UP

THUNDERSTORM

Can you write nine different verbs using only letters found in the word "thunderstorm"? Write each verb in a rain cloud.

RIDDLE ME

Use the clues to write a letter in each box in the center of the circle. You will form a common idiom.

Skill: Idioms

1. I am the letter often used to make words plural.
2. I am the 16th letter of the alphabet.
7. I am often a silent letter at the end of a word.
6. I am the silent letter in "doubt."
3. I am a letter that can also be a pronoun.
10. I am the same as the first letter.
8. I am the first letter in the alphabet.
5. I am the same as the letter before me.
9. I look like one half of the letter "m."
4. I am the first letter of a synonym for "giggle."

1	2	3	4	5

the

6	7	8	9	10

MIRROR

Skill: Subject-Verb Agreement

1. The team crowd around the coach.

2. Jonas hits the ball.

3. He slide into second base.

4. Mom, Dad, and Will claps for him.

5. The Tigers has not scored yet.

Use a mirror to read each sentence. If the subject (noun or nouns that the sentence is about) and verb agree, draw a happy face (☺) in the box. If the subject and verb do not agree, draw a sad face (☹).

Not Your Usual Workbook · Grade 3

Use the code to find the secret words. Then, decode the category for all the words.

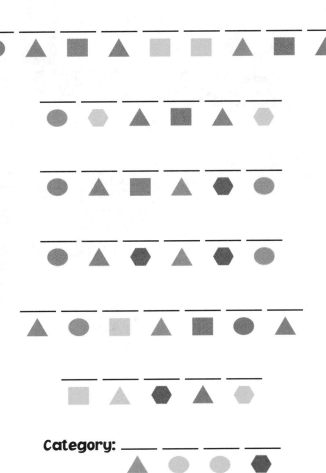

Category: ___ ___ ___ ___

CODE BREAKER

Skills: Spelling, Vocabulary

Code Key

A	B	C	D	E	F	G	H	I	J	K	L	M
▲	⬡	●	■	▲	⬡	●	■	▲	⬡	●	■	▲

N	O	P	Q	R	S	T	U	V	W	X	Y	Z
⬡	●	■	▲	⬡	●	■	▲	⬡	●	■	▲	⬡

How are bats and birds similar? How are they different? Cut out the labels. Glue or tape them in the correct places on the Venn diagram.

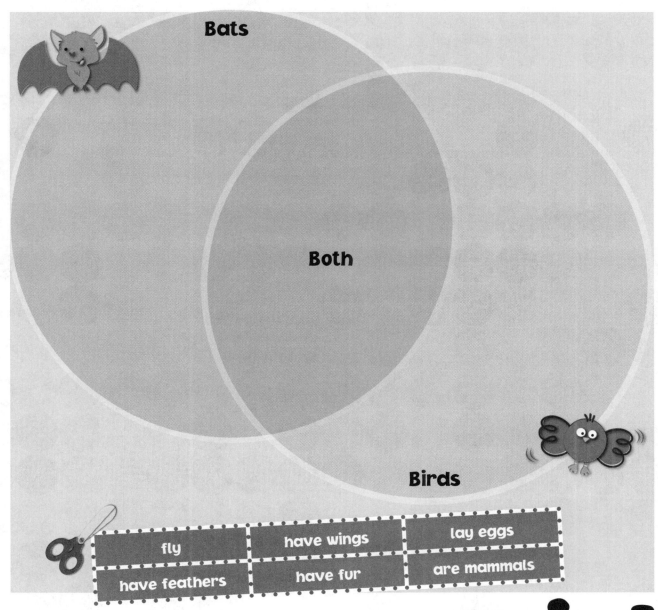

Bats

Both

Birds

| fly | have wings | lay eggs |
| have feathers | have fur | are mammals |

Picture This!

In Search Of

Skill: Parts of Speech

Find some (but not all) of these words. Hint: The words in the puzzle are all the same part of speech.

farmer
hoeing
raked
apples
planted
fertilize
natural
pruning
carrots
dirt
watered
topsoil
harvesting
pests
weeding

```
D X N D K B O S R E J A X G D
M E Z Z A N Y X V L I W B N E
T Q T E K U L J E I X W C I R
O J M N O G D Z P C I G M T E
Y T F Z A G I K O Q R B R S T
D R M H V L N G Z I M K Q E A
F H S U I Y P I Y N K H R V W
I C H T G N I D E E W X K R A
C R R S M Y P W A O C M F A I
B E C Y M R Y Z H Z H B V H N
F J C I U D H A P K L Z Y Z F
S X T N Z E M J L I S G I C I
T D I Z W T M J Y A F M S S K
K N R A K E D Q Y Y N O V U X
G W Q J J D H G H U C Y G D O
```

All the words in the puzzle are _____ !

WORD MATH

Skill: Types of Sentences

Choose one word or end mark from each box. Add the words and end mark together to make a sentence. Repeat to make more sentences. Use each word and end mark only once. You will make one statement, one question, one command, and one exclamation. Write the sentences on page 133.

| Come | Where | You're | The |

➕

| trail | is | ride | going |

➕

| with | too | my | is |

➕

| fast | bike | bumpy | me |

➕

| ? | . | . | ! |

Statement:

_____

_____

Question:

_____

_____

Command:

_____

_____

Exclamation:

_____

_____

Sudoku for you

R				
				E
		C		
	T			
			A	

Skill: Prefixes

Write letters in the spaces so that no letter appears twice in the same row or column. Do not guess. Use logic! Hint: The letters spell a word that has the prefix "re-."

What adjectives describe a fun day at the park? Write an adjective that begins with each letter. Some are provided for you.

Skill: Adjectives

Fun at the Park

A _____

B ____ busy ____

C _____

D _____

E ____ great ____

F _____

G _____

H _____

I _____

J _____

K _____

L _____

M _____

N ____ noisy ____

O _____

P _____

Q _____

R _____

S _____

T _____

U _____

V _____

W ____ warm ____

X _____

Y _____

Z _____

ALPHA-
CHALLENGE

GO ON ACROSS

The answer to each clue is a possessive noun. Each answer includes an apostrophe (') before "s" to show one animal owner or after "s" to show two animal owners. One is done for you.

²Cats'

Across

2. ____ babies are called "kittens."
4. A ____ main food source is krill, a tiny ocean creature.
5. An ____ waste, called "castings," helps create healthy soil.
8. An ____ trunk is used for drinking and picking up things.
10. ____ hooves should be trimmed and cleaned regularly.

Down

1. A ____ home in the wild is in China.
3. A ____ young are squirmy, worm-like maggots.
6. A ____ stinger is used only when it feels threatened.
7. The entrance to an ____ home is a tiny hole in the ground.
9. Male ____ manes show other lions how healthy and strong they are.

Sentence Scramble

Draw lines to connect the boxes and create cause-and-effect sentences. Write your own sentence ending in the blank box.

and dropped her lunch tray.

I could not open the door

Because the weather is nice,

Jade tripped on her shoelace

so I walked to school.

Dad's truck would not start,

because I lost the key.

Skill: Adjectives

Read the adjective inside each flower. On the petals, write nouns that each adjective could describe.

Picture This!

Write each jumbled book title correctly. Don't forget to use capital letters where needed!

csarlo'htte wbe

yrhra toptre

lttie sehuo ni eht gib swodo

prtee nap

eth wrdzai fo zo

onrama het epst

hte cboarx ilcnhdre

In Search Of

Find and circle these music words:

- treble
- melody
- harp
- piano
- tempo
- violin
- octave
- duet
- maracas
- drum
- chord

MIRROR

Write a word with the prefix "un-".

Write a word with the suffix "-ful".

Write a word with the word root "graph".

Write a word with the suffix "-ly".

Write a word with the word root "meter".

Write a word with the prefix "in-".

Use a mirror to read the directions.
Write a word that fits the description in each box.

141

Q: _____

A: It is a feeling of wanting to know more about something.

Q: _____

A: It is an emotion you feel when you are in danger.

Q: _____

A: It is a quality that helps you when you are afraid.

Q: _____

A: It is a feeling of caring and liking.

Q: _____

A: It is a state of being calm and quiet.

Write a question to go with each answer. Each question should include a word from the word box.

Word Box

curiosity

bravery

peace

fear

affection

Skill: Abstract Nouns

QUIZ WHIZ

Please

The train

Where

I

Skill: Types of Sentences

IN PIECES

Cut out the pieces. Match train engines and cars to make complete sentences. You will make one statement, one question, one command, and one exclamation.

is the station?

hand me my suitcase.

forgot my ticket!

leaves at five o'clock.

How many words can you make from the letters in the puzzle? Move in any direction from letter to letter to spell words. You may reuse a letter, but you must move to another letter first before coming back to the same letter. Try to find at least one of each: noun, verb, adjective, adverb. Write the words on the lines.

MAZE CRAZE

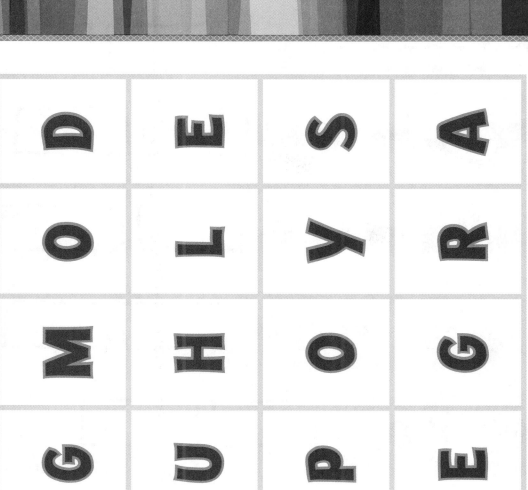

G	M	O	D
U	H	L	E
P	O	Y	S
E	G	R	A

WORD
MATH
Skill: Plurals

Solve each word puzzle. Write your answer in the first box and the plural of the word in the second box.

1. 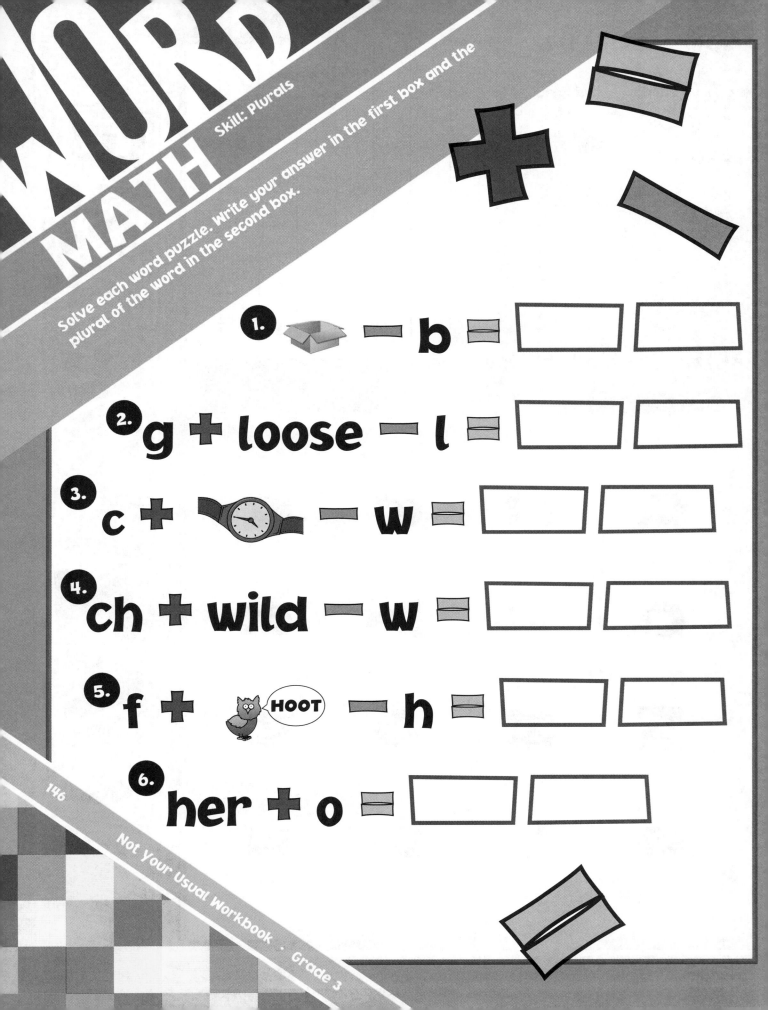 − b =

2. g + loose − l =

3. c + 🕐 − w =

4. ch + wild − w =

5. f + 🦉 (HOOT) − h =

6. her + o =

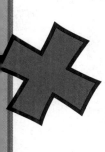

7. c + ⬤ − h = ☐ ☐

8. toots − s + h = ☐ ☐

9. p + reach − r = ☐ ☐

10. STORE − e + y = ☐ ☐

11. lead − d + f = ☐ ☐

12. 🐭 − u + o = ☐ ☐

RIDDLE ME

Answer each riddle. Then, write the first letter of each answer to reveal a secret word.

Skill: Context Clues

If the moon were made of cheese, what would the holes be? ___ ___ r

a ___ ___ ___ n

Where do space cows travel? in the ___ ___ r

Which planet gets lots of phone calls?

x ___ ___ e

Why is the sun so famous? because it is a big ___ ___ y

What should you pack to help you breathe deeply and relax? ___ ___ r

On a trip to space, what should you pack to help you breathe deeply and relax? ___ v ___

Where could you find glasses powerful enough to see into space? at an ___ ___ b

Secret Word

Sentence Scramble

Draw a line to connect the sentences in the correct order to tell a story.

The bird ate breakfast.

The bird flew from its nest.

The bird returned to its nest.

The bird looked for breakfast.

The bird found a fat, juicy worm.

PREST-O

CHANGE-O!

Skill: Nouns

Does it take magic to turn a coat into a shoe? No, you just need to change one letter at a time! Write a noun to match each clue. Each word should be the same as the word above it except for one changed letter.

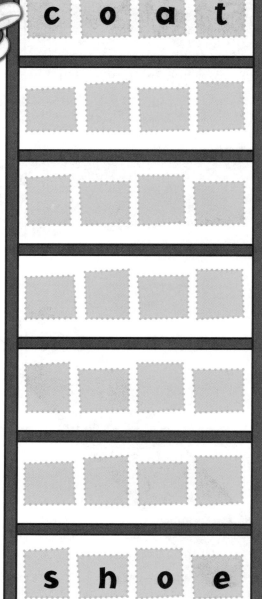

c o a t

a talk or discussion

a British fellow

made from a potato

a big boat

a place for selling

s h o e

JUMBLED UP

Secret Word:

Unscramble each group of letters to spell a possessive pronoun. The circled letters spell a secret word.

nmie

rysou

sih

esirth

ersh

osru

uoyr

GO ON ACROSS

Fill in the puzzle with a verb that fits each blank. Decide if the verb should be in the present, past, or future tense. Hint: Three answers will have two words.

Across

1. I ___ the dog yesterday.
4. The bird ___ south every November.
6. After it ___ this morning, I saw a pretty rainbow.
7. Abraham Lincoln ___ more than 150 years ago.
8. ___ the other end of this rope.

Down

1. I ___ a letter to my grandfather tomorrow.
2. My sister ___ her bike outside right now.
3. Please ___ your room.
5. Hector ___ the piano later this evening.

CODE BREAKER

Skill: Word Roots

Use the code to find words in each group that share a word root. Write each word root beside its definition.

Word Root: _____ = to break

_____

_____

_____

Word Root: _____ = drag or pull

_____

_____

_____

Code Key

A	B	C	D	E	F	G	H	I	J	K	L	M
▲	⬡	●	■	▲	⬡	●	■	▲	⬡	●	■	▲

N	O	P	Q	R	S	T	U	V	W	X	Y	Z
⬡	●	■	▲	⬡	●	■	▲	⬡	●	■	▲	⬡

Skills: Collective Nouns, Subject-Verb Agreement

Collective nouns name groups of animals, people, or things. Draw a line from each collective noun to what it describes.

bunch

herd

swarm

crowd

pack

OF

wolves

bees

cows

flowers

people

Now, choose two collective nouns. Use each as the subject of a present-tense sentence. Hint: A collective noun describes a group, but it is a singular noun and needs a singular verb.

_____

_____

_____

_____

Picture This!

In Search Of

Find these conjunctions, or joining words:

- and
- unless
- although
- for
- because
- while
- but
- yet
- after
- nor
- since
- until

Skill: Idioms

An idiom is a well-known phrase whose meaning is different from the literal meanings of the words that make it up. Solve each puzzle. Write the idiom and its meaning.

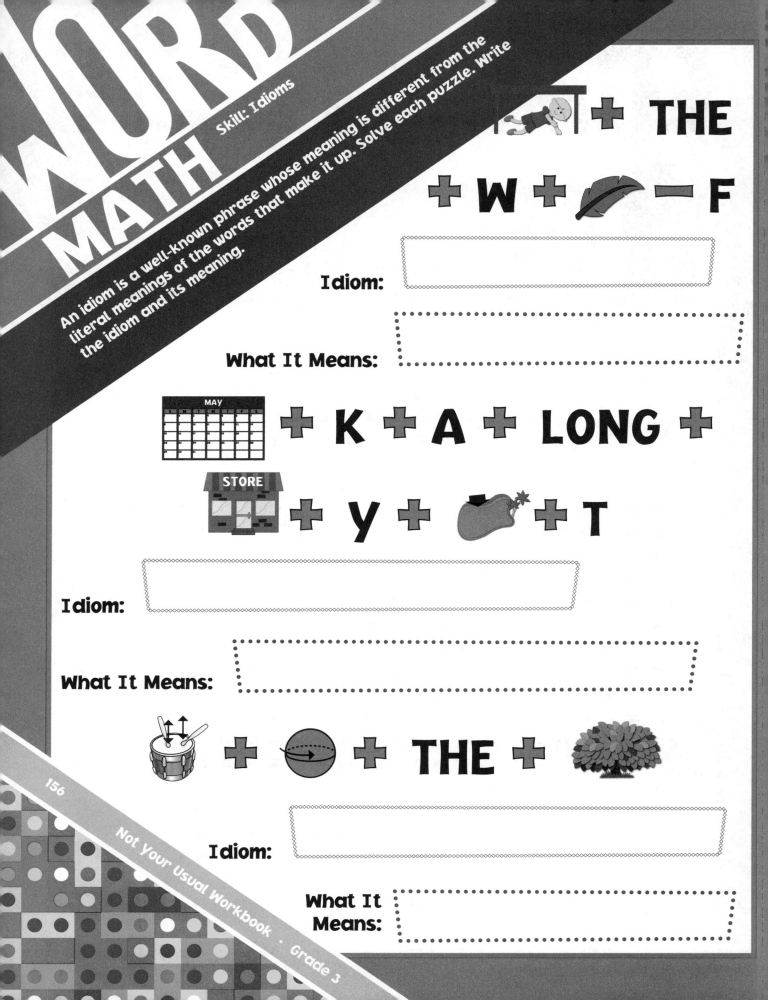

[baby crawling] + **THE** + **W** + [feather] − **F**

Idiom:

What It Means:

[MAY calendar] + **K** + **A** + **LONG** + [STORE] + **y** + [bomb] + **T**

Idiom:

What It Means:

[drum] + [ball] + **THE** + [bush]

Idiom:

What It Means:

+ **THE** +  **– S** +

+ **THE** +

Idiom:

What It Means:

 + + **THE** +

– RUBBER +

Idiom:

What It Means:

Write the letters that make up a word in the spaces so that no letter appears twice in the same row or column. Do not guess. Use logic! Then, write the word:

		D		
U				A
	G			R

Sudoku for you

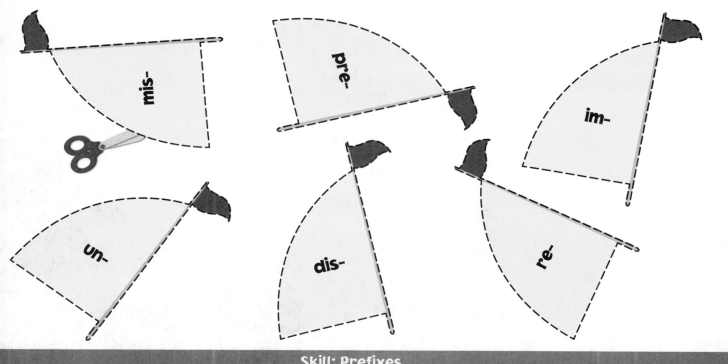

IN PIECES

Cut out the pieces. Match each prefix with a base word to complete the sailboats.

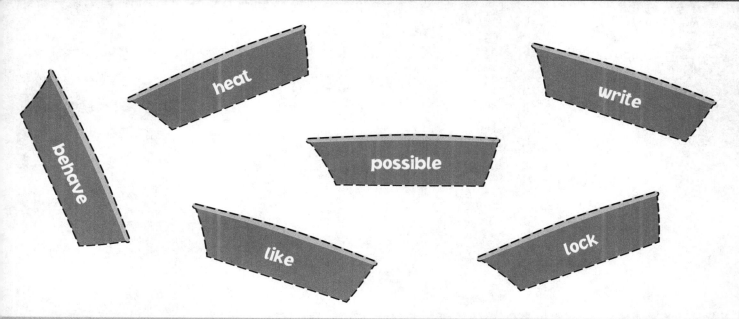

RIDDLE ME

Write a letter for each clue. Put the letters together to write the answer to the riddle.

Skill: Spelling

1. This letter is in [pan] but not in [mop]

2. This letter is in [cap] but not in [bat]

3. This letter is in [fan] but not in [shark]

4. This letter is in [shark] but not in [fan]

5. This letter is in [boat] but not in [bucket]

I travel all over the world but always stay in my corner. I am a . . .

☐ ☐ ☐ ☐ ☐

Fill in the chart. Write words that begin with each letter shown and that match each part of speech. Some are given for you.

Skill: Parts of Speech

Part of Speech	Letter: R	Letter: B	Letter: T	Letter: S
Common Noun				
Proper Noun				Samantha
Abstract Noun				
Verb			tugged	
Adjective	red			
Adverb		bravely		

ALPHA-
CHALLENGE

JUMBLED UP

Lincoln

backward.

I

never

said

slowly

walk

Abraham

walk

but

I

Rearrange the words to make a complete sentence. It will contain a famous quote. When your write the sentence on the lines, be sure to add commas and quotation marks where they are needed.

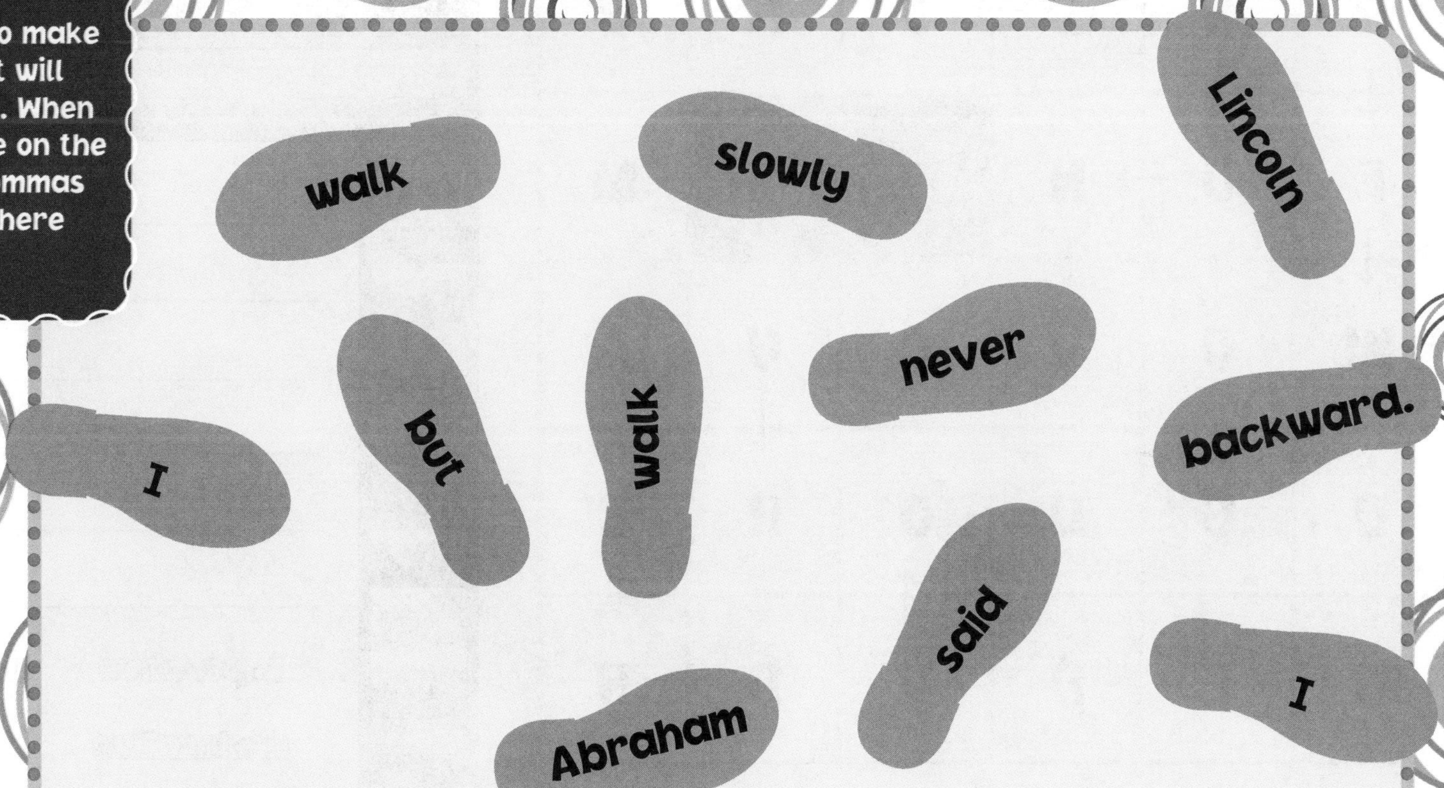

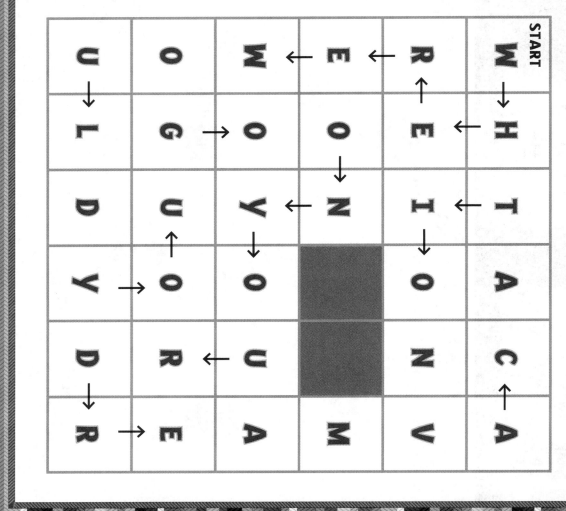

START

Skill: Types of Sentences

Begin at START. Follow the arrows to find a secret sentence. Write it on the lines. Be sure to add the correct capitalization and punctuation to your sentence. Then, circle the type of sentence you have written.

imperative   interrogative

declarative   exclamatory

Not Your Usual Workbook · Grade 3

GO ON ACROSS

²GO⁶A
⁴ON
S

Write the plural
of each word. Then, fit
the plurals you wrote
into the puzzle.

man: _____ _____ _____

sheep: _____ _____ _____

person: _____ _____ _____

child: _____ _____ _____

cherry: _____ _____ _____

wolf: _____ _____ _____

fox: _____ _____ _____

girl: _____ _____ _____

fish: _____ _____ _____

PREST-O CHANGE-O!

Skill: Vocabulary

Write words to match the clues. Each word you write will be the same as the word above it with the addition of one new letter.

an article **a**

My mom's _____ work today.

rodent bigger than a mouse

give a movie five stars, perhaps

very angry

a swashbuckler

stolen

IN PIECES

Cut out the pieces. Match the trunks and treetops to show two forms of each irregular verb.

Write each word on a fish below its matching prefix, word root, or suffix.

unlock	undo	unreal	illness
perimeter	baldness	fitness	greatness
geometry	thermometer	unsafe	millimeter

un-   meter   -ness

Picture This!

Write a sentence with a five-letter noun, a five-letter verb, and a five-letter adjective.

_____

_____

Rearrange the letters in "pots" to make a verb. Use both words in a sentence.

_____

_____

Use letters from "please" to make a noun and a verb. Use the new words in a sentence.

_____

_____

A palindrome is spelled the same backward or forward, like "pop." Write a sentence with two palindromes.

_____

_____

How good are you at following directions? Write the sentences described to find out!

QUIZ WHIZ

Skills: Parts of Speech, Spelling

MIRROR

1. The world is your oyster.

   _____

2. Ms. Antonelli bent over backward to help us.

   _____

3. My friend was tickled pink to get a new bike.

   _____

4. Sam lied, and now he is really in a pickle.

   _____

5. Keep the surprise party a secret. Try not to let the cat out of the bag.

   _____

Use a mirror to see the reversed word in each idiom. Write it on the line.

Skill: Adjectives

Write the adjective shown by the picture in each rebus puzzle.

1. a  jacket

2. |||| kittens

3. a sky

4. a porcupine

5. a boy

6. a  afternoon

[ ]

7. a pencil

[ ]

8. a pizza

[ ]

9. a shirt

[ ]

10. soup

[ ]

MAZE CRAZE

proudly	fairly	his	pencil	or	juice
green	easily	gently	sweep	pool	angry
read	but	soon	cute	flower	and
me	kite	never	jump	tomato	sweet
laugh	furry	calmly	lazily	twirl	six
pie	catch	fence	always	deeply	slowly

Skill: Adverbs

Cross out each adverb to help the ant find a path to the picnic basket. Then, write your own adverbs on the lines.

_____
_____
_____
_____
_____
_____
_____

CODE BREAKER

Skills: Context Clues, Subject-Verb Agreement

A famous quote from Dr. Seuss is written below in code. Can you crack the code? Use the hints to help you get started. Keep track of each letter using the chart.

Gsv nliv gszg blf ovzim, gsv nliv kozxvh blf'oo tl.

___ ____ ____ ____

___ ____ _____ ,

___ _____ _____ ,

____ ___ .

Hints: (Verbs are in the present tense.)

The children **hdrn** at the neighborhood pool.

___ ___ ___

Lance **krgxsvh** on the mound for our baseball team.

___ ___ ___ ___ ___ ___ ___

The parents **xsvvi** loudly for their children's team.

___ ___ ___ ___ ___

We bounce in our saddles as the horses **tzoolk**.

___ ___ ___ ___ ___ ___

Code Key

A	B	C	D	E	F	G	H	I	J	K	L	M

N	O	P	Q	R	S	T	U	V	W	X	Y	Z

Sentence Scramble

Draw a line to connect the words and form a sentence. Write the sentence at the bottom of the page. Be sure to add a comma where it belongs.

his

teacher

"The

brother

my

ate

dog

homework!"

My

told

_____

_____

We climbed the hill_____.

_____ I missed the party.

The sun shone brightly_____.

_____ we ran out of gas.

Someone knocked on the door_____.

Finish the sentences. Write a cause for each effect. Write an effect for each cause. Award yourself points for using the words in the word box.

Word Box

so = 1 point
because = 2 points
therefore = 3 points
consequently = 4 points

My point total: _____

Skill: Cause and Effect

QUIZ WHIZ

Skill: Verbs

Find the past-tense form of each verb:

- go
- hold
- break
- race
- fly
- choose
- begin
- grow
- read
- stir
- paint
- chop

Sudoku for you

				O
			F	
C				
	E			

Skill: Vocabulary

Write letters in the spaces so that each row and column contains the letters to spell a five-letter word that means "a push or a pull." No letter should appear twice in the same row or column. Do not guess. Use logic!

Write the word here:

_____

JUMBLED UP

SILHOUETTE

How many smaller words can you make from the letters in "silhouette"? Write the words on the lines.

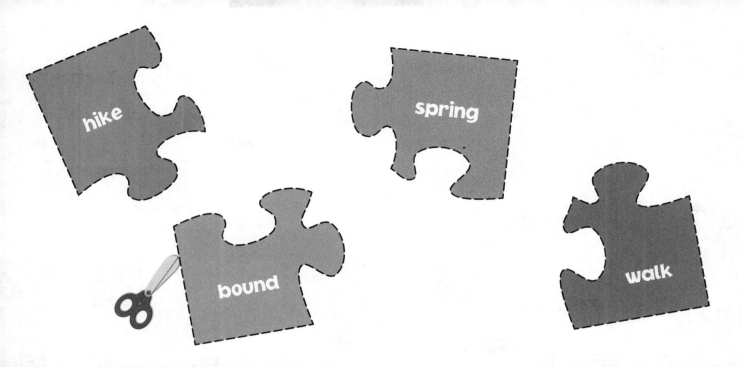

IN PIECES

Synonyms are words that have the same or nearly the same meaning. Cut out the pieces. Put them together to make two separate squares containing verbs that are synonyms.

Skill: Prefixes

GO ON ACROSS

Across

3. not possible

5. not able

6. made before

7. seal again

Down

1. does not agree

2. read again

3. not proper

4. view before

5. not fair

Write four different sentences about your favorite movie. Crack the code to find out which type of sentence to write each time!

CODE BREAKER

Skill: Types of Sentences

Code Key

A	B	C	D	E	F	G	H	I	J	K	L	M

N	O	P	Q	R	S	T	U	V	W	X	Y	Z

MAZE CRAZE

Skill: Possessives

Cross out each possessive pronoun in the puzzle to help the dog find the bone. Then, choose two words you crossed out. Use them to write sentences on the lines.

mine	he	then	they	an	but
yours	what	his	its	theirs	all
theirs	ours	hers	its	the	it
and	is	will	or	ours	mine
she	because	or	never	is	its
soon	it	now	can't	a	his

Who am I? _____

What do I say? _____

Who am I? _____

What do I say? _____

Who am I? _____

What do I say? _____

Who am I? _____

What do I say? _____

Choose four famous people from the box and write their names in the spaces above. If you were each of these people, what would your point of view be? What would you say? Write a sentence that each person might say. Your sentences can be silly or serious.

Amelia Earhart   Paul Revere

George Washington   Jackie Robinson

Susan B. Anthony   Abraham Lincoln

Albert Einstein   Harriet Tubman

QUIZ WHIZ

Skill: Point of View

Some words can be more than one part of speech. For example, "dance" can be a noun (Let's go to the dance together). It can also be a verb (We dance to our favorite song). Write each word in the correct place in the Venn diagram.

check	marble	actor	imagine	point	throne
crash	consider	jellyfish	lean	cellar	hike
adopt	hug	cactus	doze	brush	believe

Nouns

Both

Verbs

Picture This!

Bowl words:
baby, quick, good, conduct, care, enjoy, subtract, play

Spoon suffixes: -tion, -ness, -ies, -ly, -ment, -ful, -less, -or

Match the base words in the bowl with the suffixes on the spoons to form new words. Write the words in the boxes. Hint: You may need to change a base word's spelling before adding the suffix.

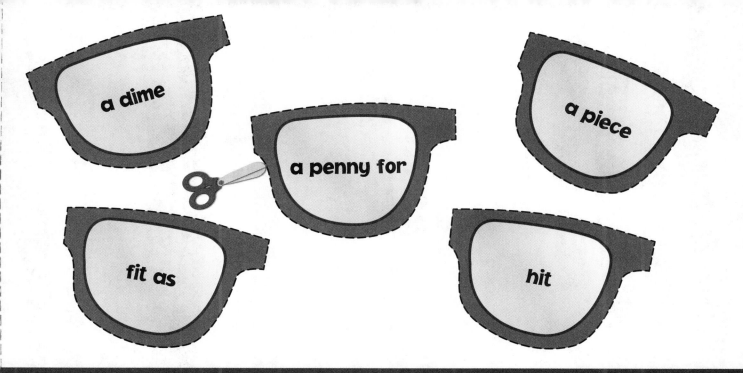

a dime

a penny for

a piece

fit as

hit

Skill: Idioms

IN PIECES

Cut out the pieces. Make pairs of glasses by matching the halves to form common sayings, or idioms.

a dozen

your thoughts

of cake

a fiddle

the road

Skill: Using Commas

Hannah Bell
1548 W. Third Ave.
San Diego CA 92093

Lila Ramirez
110 Oakhurst Ln.
Madison WI 53711

Derek Mefti
71552 Linville Rd.
Baltimore MD 21218

These letters cannot be delivered! Use a mirror to read each address and write it correctly. Include commas where they are needed.

Sentence Scramble

Draw lines to connect the words in the correct order to form four different sentences. On the line, write "S" for simple sentences, "C" for compound sentences, or "CX" for complex sentences.

Although the bird is a fledgling,

Amina is training

to run a marathon. _____

it still depends on its mother. _____

build a tree house with Dad. _____

The storm started at 2:00,

and we lost power at 2:30. _____

Cameron wants to

Read the phrases. Write each purple word in the correct balloon.

Sarah's **gift**
the **balloons'** strings
the **cake's** candles
the **guests'** favors

the **banner's** flags
Ana's **plate**

the **kids'** hats
Marco's **games**
the **girls'** dresses
the **party's** invitations

Plurals

Plural Possessives

Possessives

Picture This!

In Search Of

Skill: Verbs

Find the past-tense form of these verbs:

write
ring
wait
brag
throw
dream
sink
judge
begin
quiz
protect
shave
beat
trap
catch
win
annoy

```
                                          F G L A D J C X
                                    G E A X N Y V H A V H R
                                U F M H A P P Y J L R U H U
                          A B J P R O T E C T E D U G D H
                          L H R C D P B Q T D E K X O F X
                    D M B W A V E U L H F E D G J Z U K I
                    Z P Q O R C G I Y R R K L R G N C Z H L I
              N S A C O M Z G E O K D I E O P A W N I T A
          I H R I Z T N Z W E P N A A H O E R V N N I T A N G W
          K Y Q Z I E Q M G A D K N W M L R K T I G A Q Z T I
    M L Q J D S H A V E D N W A E G F K S T P L E A S E
    F Z T A N A G E B B E A T F D W V Z I K P Y R J H N
    D C V J T G R J N C N S N I D I O E M B O V C K T D
    Q D P X L Q F S I A I C E E N N L G F T H L Y
    A L W U F T D P H I U G I U W I I U W R
    Q K E D E P P A R T D G B L D I Y O H A
    H G R Z B B W U L Y H H P R P S W
    P J G L P P J I G Q N T M D C E
    S N M C B R X Y P O M Z J O
    P F X E J T K O X A K M
    H O P E F U L I Y
```

PREST-O CHANGE-O!

Skill: Vocabulary

Can you change fear into hope? Yes, you can! Just change one letter at a time. Write a word that is a synonym for each word shown. Each word you write should be the same as the word above it except for one changed letter.

accomplishment

celebration

speedy

actors

container

cloak

manage

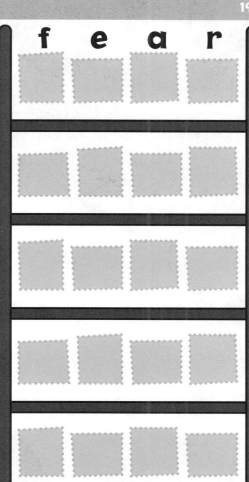

f e a r

h o p e

RIDDLE ME

Solve the clues. Write the letters where they belong to find the mystery word.

Skill: Spelling

1. The first letter is in [image] but not in [image]

2. The second letter is in [image] but not in [image]

3. The third letter is in [image] but not in [image]

4. The fourth letter is in [image] but not in [image]

5. The fifth letter is in [image] and in [image]

6. The sixth letter is in [image] but not in [image]

7. The seventh letter is in [image] and in [image]

The mystery word is:

1	2	3	4	5	6	7

GO ON ACROSS

Skill: Cause and Effect

Each clue describes an effect. Identify the cause and write it in the puzzle. Hint: All of the answers are weather words.

Across

2. You put on your shades.

4. You open an umbrella.

5. You hear thunder.

7. You have to shovel the sidewalk.

Down

1. You decide to go fly a kite.

2. You see flowers and baby birds.

3. You rush to the basement to seek shelter.

6. You begin to sweat.

Skill: Adverbs

Adverbs describe verbs. They might tell where, when, or how something is happening. Many adverbs end in "ly." Write an adverb that begins with each letter of the alphabet. Some are given for you.

Adverbs

A above

B

C

D

E

F fairly

G

H

I

J

K

L

M

N

O

P

Q

R

S

T tearfully

U

V

W

X

Y yesterday

Z

ALPHA-
CHALLENGE

JUMBLED UP

MYSTERIOUS MUSTACHE

How many pronouns can you write using only the letters found in "mysterious mustache"? Write each word in a mustache.

Skill: Point of View

Decode each sentence and write it in the box. Then, in the yellow box, write "F" if the sentence is written from a first-person point of view. If it is written from a third-person point of view, write "T."

1.  r + – f 2 the store 4 a of + za.

2. K + – g l + – b 2 b + – r .

3.  l + 📖 − b 🐱 − c U + r 🏠 + work?

[answer box]

4. M + 👁 d + 🐸 − fr 🥫 🐱 + ch a Fris + 🐝.

[answer box]

5. H + 🐄 − c  − g will R + 🪶 − st 🐝 2 + day?

[answer box]

RIDDLE ME

Solve the clues. Write the letters in the boxes to find a common word root.
Then, write words on the lines that contain the root.

Skill: Word Roots

1. I am the first letter of the green covering in your yard.

2. I am the first letter of a synonym for "very impolite."

3. I am the first letter of the alphabet.

4. My mirror image looks like the letter "q."

5. My capital looks like one rung of a ladder.

| 1 | 2 | 3 | 4 | 5 |

_____   _____

_____   _____

_____   _____

How many words of three letters or more can you find in the puzzle? Move in any direction from letter to letter to spell words. You may reuse a letter, but you must move to another letter first before coming back to the same letter. Write the words on the lines.

MAZE CRAZE

D	R	S	B
C	A	T	O
P	H	I	A
W	E	G	N

WORD MATH

Skills: Conjunctions, Writing Sentences

An easy way to remember seven conjunctions is to think of the acronym "FAN Boys." Solve each rebus puzzle. Write the conjunction you find. Then, combine each pair of sentences using one of the conjunctions you wrote.

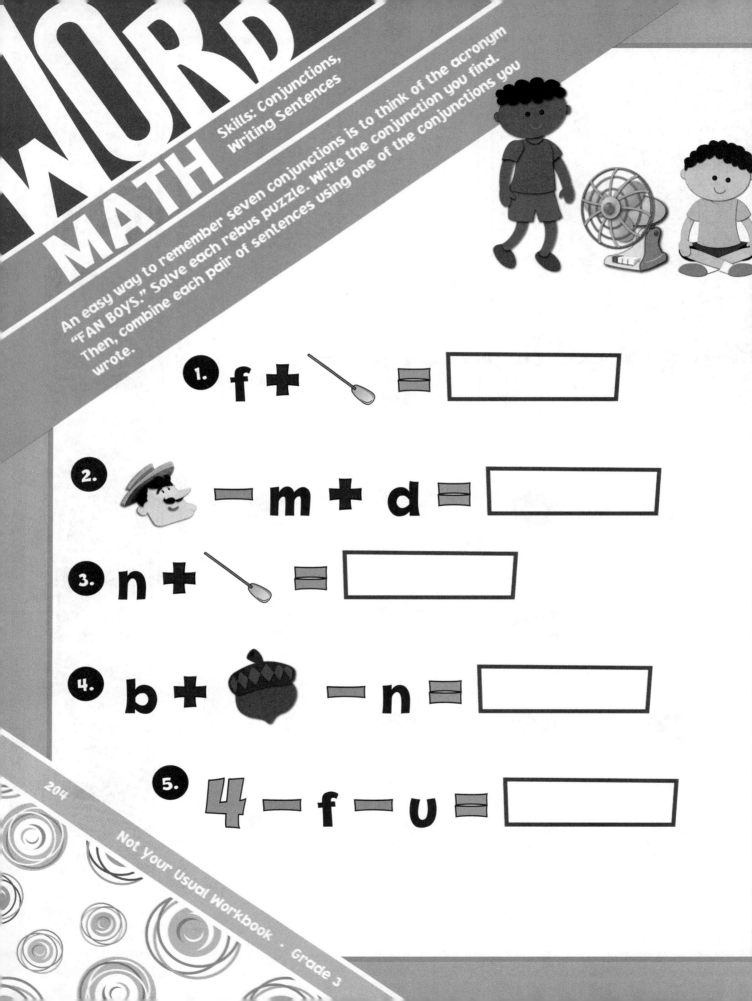

1. f + 🥄 = [_____]

2. 👳 − m + d = [_____]

3. n + 🥄 = [_____]

4. b + 🌰 − n = [_____]

5. 4 − f − u = [_____]

6. y + 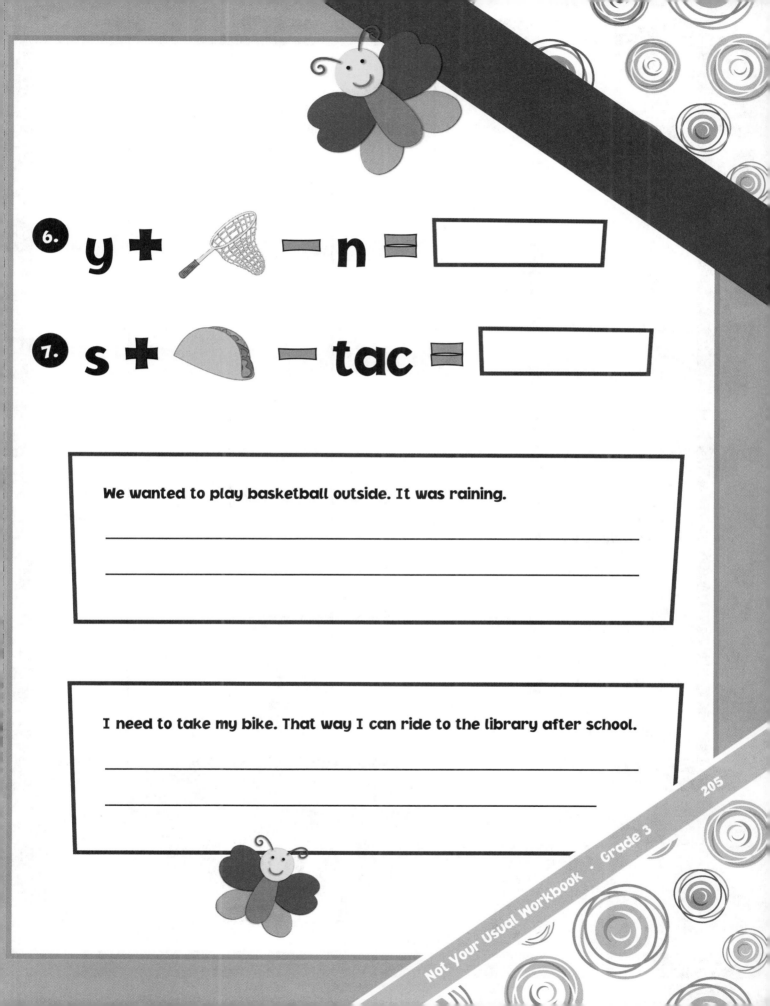 − n = ☐

7. s + ☐ − tac = ☐

We wanted to play basketball outside. It was raining.

_____

_____

I need to take my bike. That way I can ride to the library after school.

_____

_____

Sudoku for you

		I		
L				
	E			
			S	

Skill: Plurals

Write letters in the spaces so that each row and column contains the letters to spell the plural form of "life." No letter should appear twice in the same row or column. Do not guess. Use logic!

Page 8

Page 9

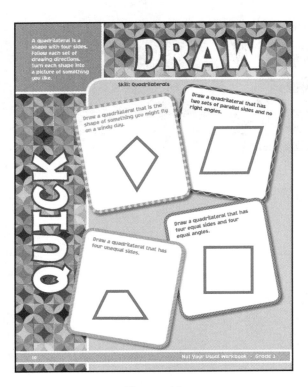

Page 10

Page 11

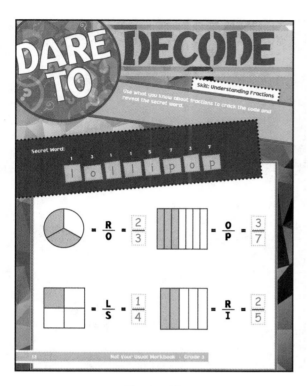

Page 12

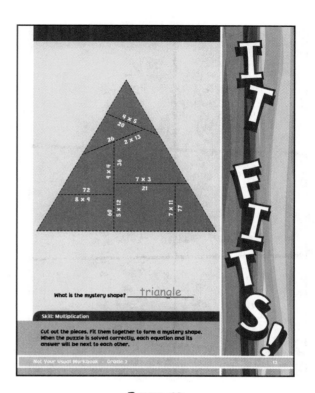

Page 13

Page 15

Page 16

Page 17

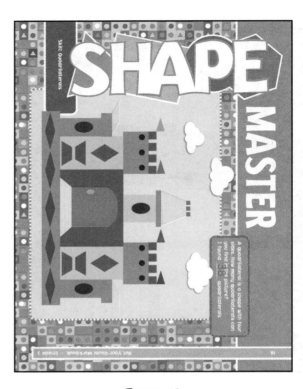

Page 18

Page 19

Page 20

Page 21

Page 23

Page 24

Page 25

Page 26

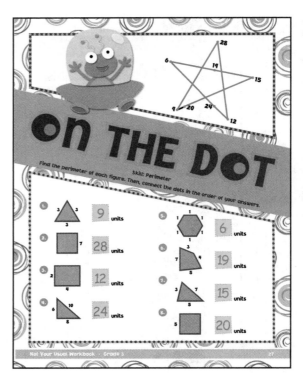

Page 27

Page 28

Page 29

Page 31

Page 32

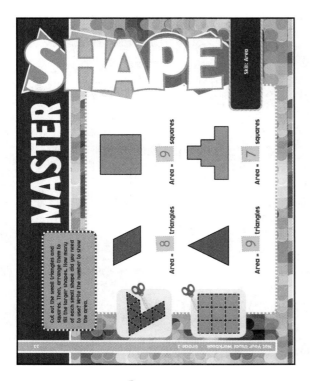

Page 33

Page 35

Page 36

Page 37

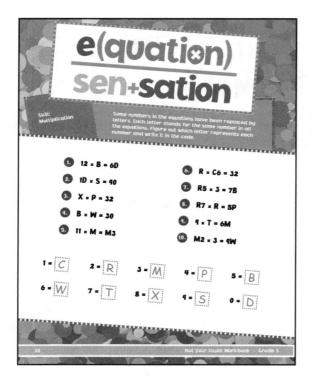

Page 38

Page 39

Page 40

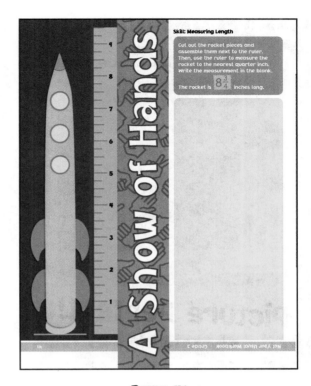

Page 41

Page 43

Page 44

Page 45

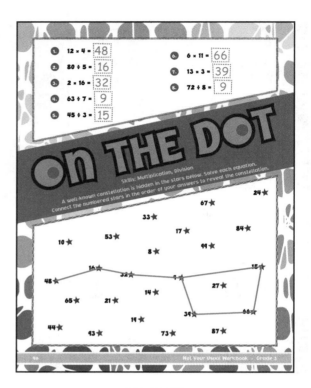

Page 46

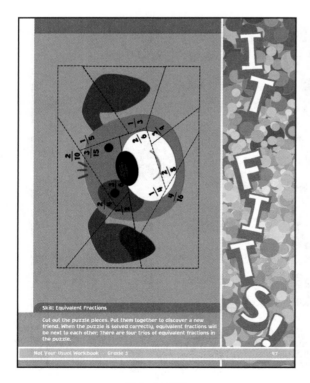

Page 47

Page 49

Page 50

Page 51

Page 52

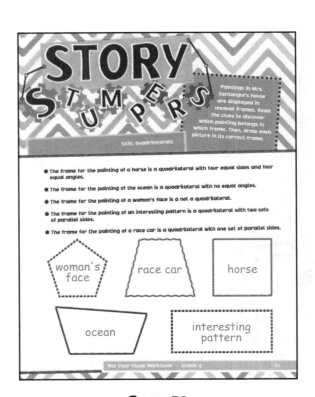

Page 53

Page 54

Page 55

Page 56

Page 57

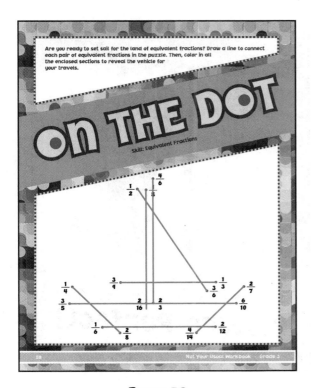

Page 58

Page 59

Page 60

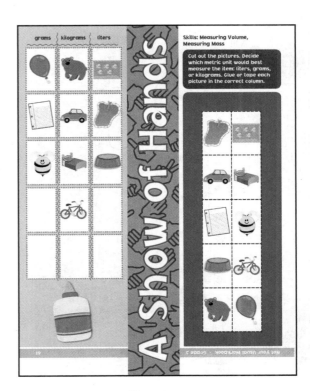

Page 61

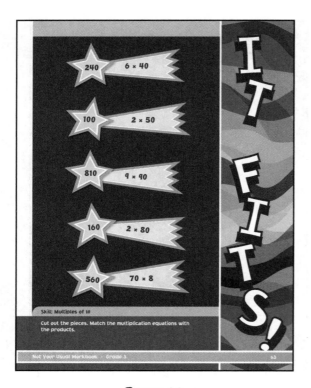

Page 63

Page 65

Page 66

Page 67

Page 68

Page 69

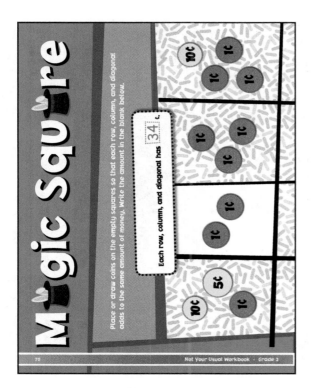

Page 70

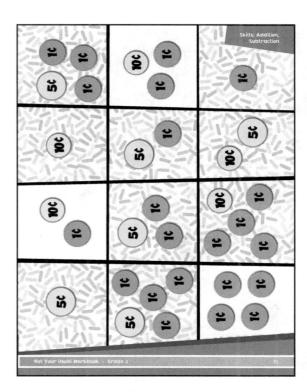

Page 71

DRAW QUICK

Use the dots to draw squares. They can be any size, and the squares can overlap. How many total squares can you draw? Write the number in the blank.

Skill: Quadrilaterals

I drew **50** squares.

Page 72

e(quation) sen+sation

Skills: Addition, Subtraction, Multiplication, Division

Each equation includes the numbers 1 through 4. Each number appears just once in each equation before the equal sign. Do the operations from left to right. Fill in the missing numbers. One is done for you.

1. $2 + \boxed{6} \times 1 - \boxed{4} \times 3 + 9 \div 7 + \boxed{8} - 5 = 55$

2. $9 + \boxed{3} - 6 \times \boxed{5} - 4 + \boxed{1} + 8 \div \boxed{7} - 2 = 3$

3. $1 + \boxed{9} \div 2 + \boxed{3} \times 7 + \boxed{8} + 4 - \boxed{5} + 6 = 12$

4. $4 \times \boxed{5} + 6 - \boxed{8} + 9 \times \boxed{2} + 1 + \boxed{7} \div 3 = 4$

5. $8 - \boxed{3} \times 5 \times \boxed{2} - 6 \div \boxed{4} + 7 - \boxed{9} \div 1 = 9$

Page 73

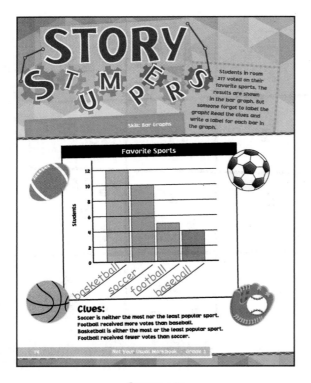

STORY STUMPERS

Skill: Bar Graphs

Students in room 217 voted on their favorite sports. The results are shown in the bar graph. But someone forgot to label the graph! Read the clues and write a label for each bar in the graph.

Favorite Sports

Students (0–12)

basketball   soccer   football   baseball

Clues:
Soccer is neither the most nor the least popular sport.
Football received more votes than baseball.
Basketball is either the most or the least popular sport.
Football received fewer votes than soccer.

Page 74

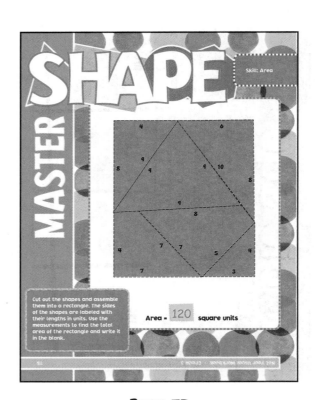

SHAPE MASTER

Skill: Area

Cut out the shapes and assemble them into a rectangle. The sides of the shapes are labeled with their lengths in units. Use the measurements to find the total area of the rectangle and write it in the blank.

Area = **120** square units

Page 75

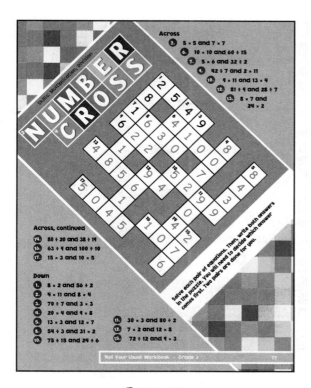

Page 77

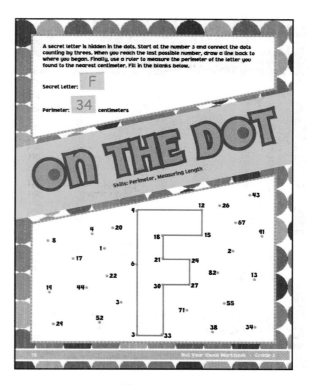

Page 78

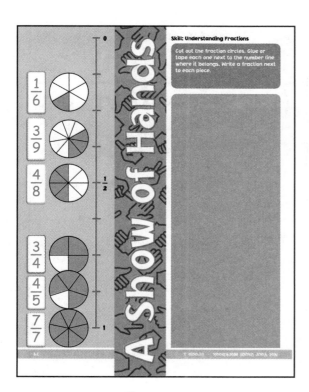

Page 79

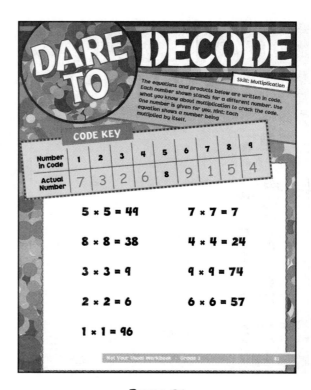

Page 81

Page 82

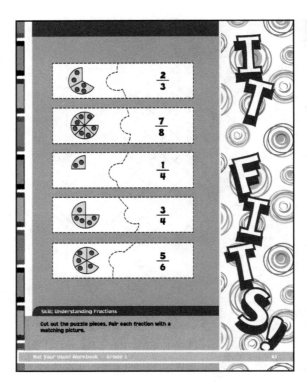

Page 83

Page 85

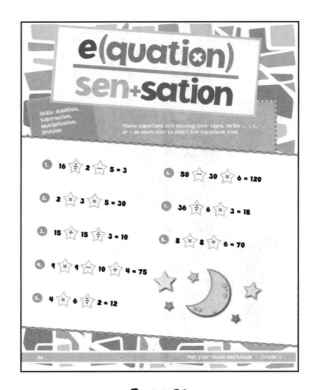

Page 86

Page 87

Page 88

Page 89

Page 90

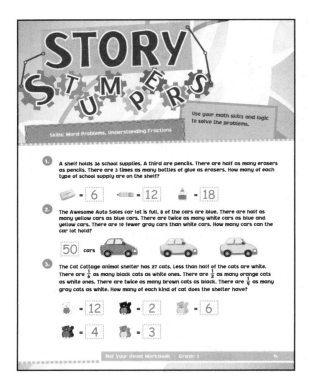

Page 91

Page 92

Page 93

Page 94

Page 95

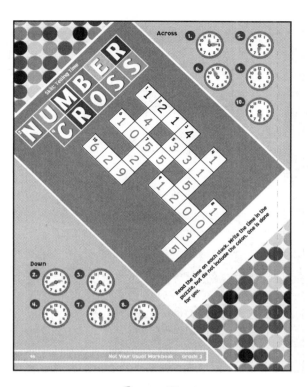

Page 96

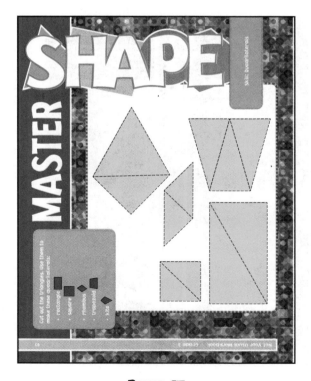

Page 97

Drawings will vary.

Page 99

Page 100

Page 101

Page 102

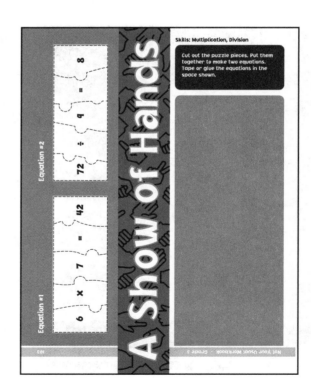

Page 103

Page 105

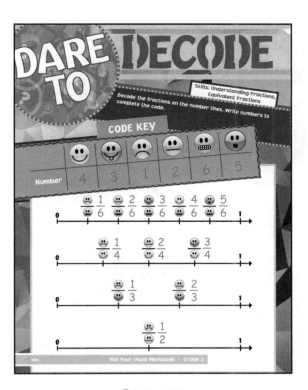

Page 106

Page 108

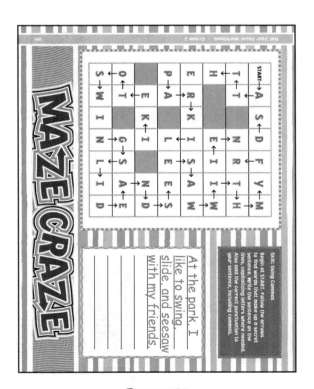

Page 109

Page 110

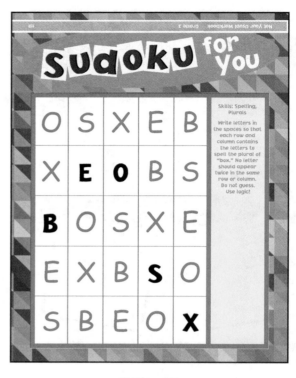

Page 111

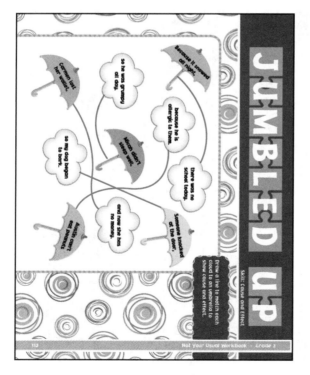

Page 112

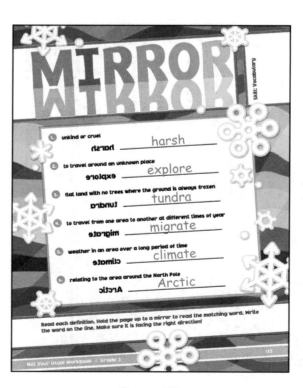

Page 113

Page 114

Page 115

Page 116

Page 117

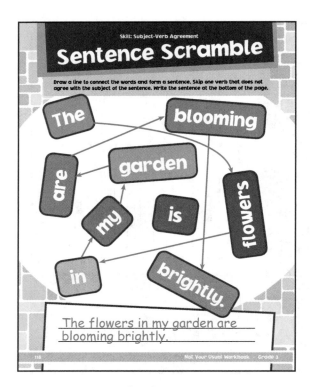

Page 118

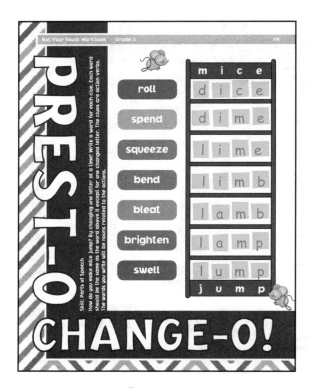

Page 119

Page 120

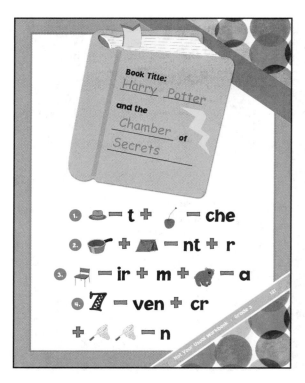

Page 121

Page 122

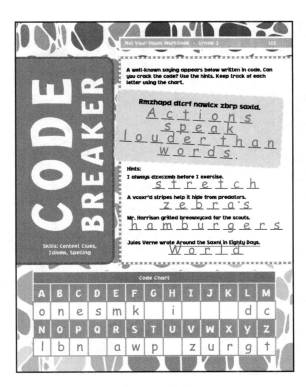

Page 123

Page 124

Page 125

Page 126

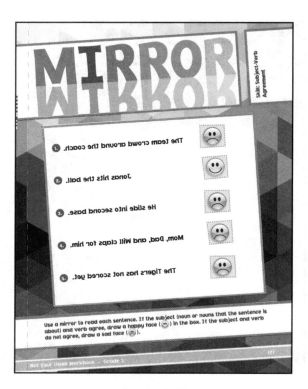

Page 127

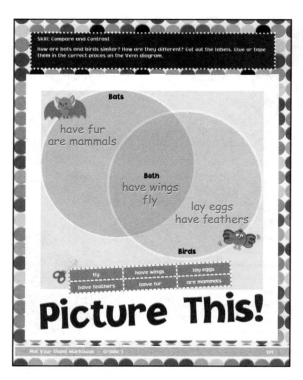

Page 128

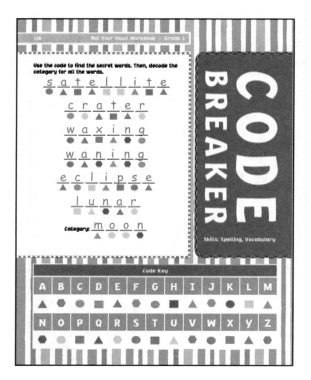

Page 129

Page 131

Page 132

Page 133

Page 134

Page 135

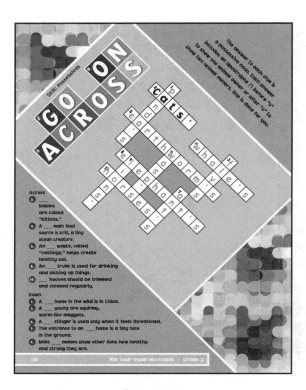

Page 136

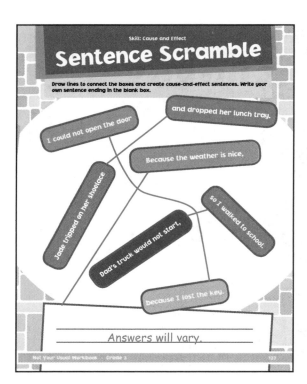

Page 137

Page 138

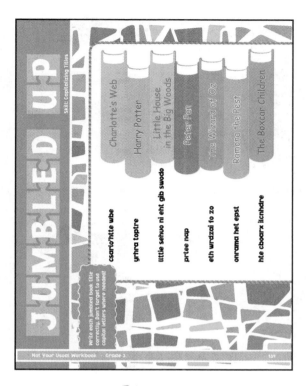

Page 139

Page 140

Page 141

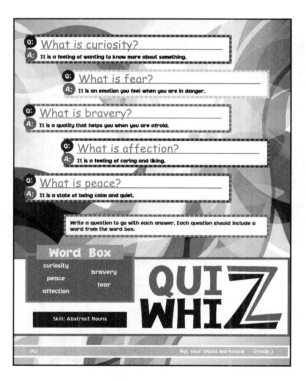

Page 142

Page 143

Page 145

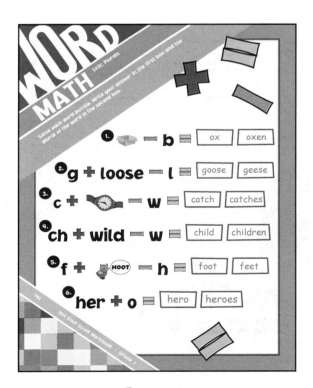

Page 146

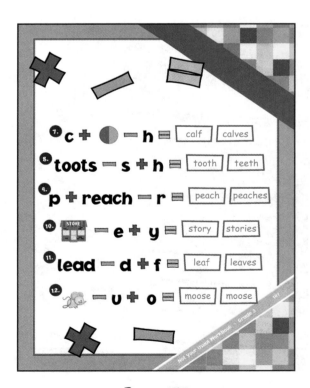

Page 147

Page 148

Page 149

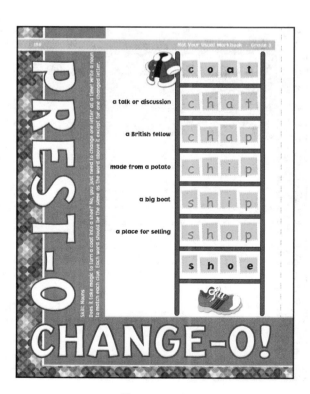

Page 150

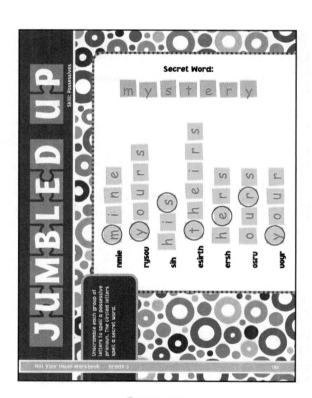

Page 151

Page 152

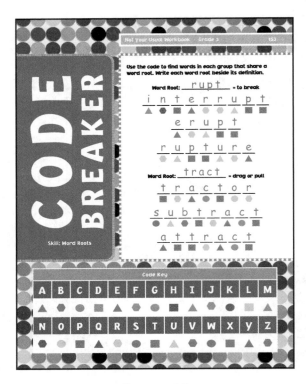

Page 153

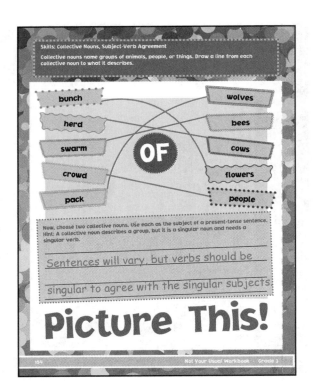

Page 154

Page 155

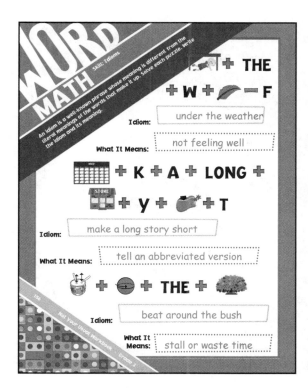

Page 156

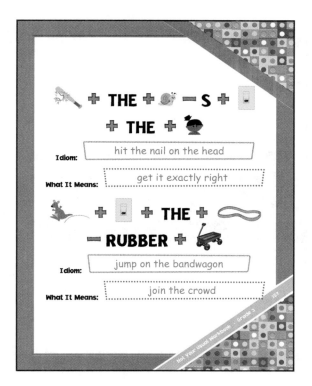

Page 157

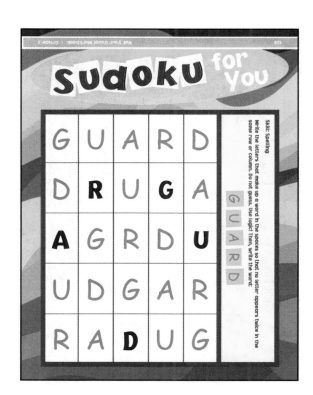

Page 158

Page 159

Page 161

Page 162

Page 163

Page 164

Page 165

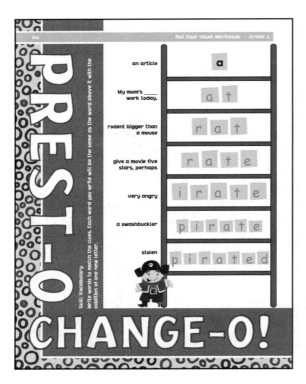

Page 166

Page 167

Page 169

Page 170

Write a sentence with a five-letter noun, a five-letter verb, and a five-letter adjective.

_____

Rearrange the letters in "pots" to make a verb. Use both words in a sentence.

_____

Use letters from "pleas_____ new words in a sentence.

_____

A palindrome is spelled the same backward or forward, like "pop." Write a sentence with two palindromes.

_____

Answers will vary.

How good are you at following directions? Write the sentences described to find out!

Skills: Parts of Speech, Spelling

QUIZ WHIZ

Page 170

Page 171

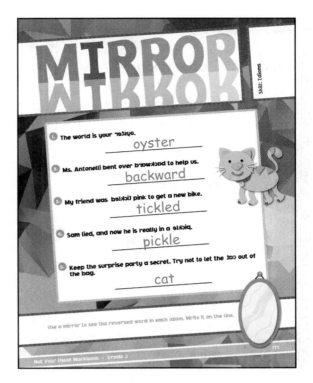

MIRROR

Skill: Idioms

1. The world is your oyster.
   oyster

2. Ms. Antonelli bent over backward to help us.
   backward

3. My friend was tickled pink to get a new bike.
   tickled

4. Sam lied, and now he is really in a pickle.
   pickle

5. Keep the surprise party a secret. Try not to let the cat out of the bag.
   cat

Use a mirror to see the reversed word in each idiom. Write it on the line.

Page 171

Page 172

WORD MATH

Skill: Adjectives

Write the adjective shown by the picture in each rebus puzzle.

1. a 🌼 jacket
   yellow

2. 卌 kittens
   five

3. a ☁☁ sky
   cloudy

4. a 🌵 porcupine
   spiky

5. a 🙂 boy
   happy

Page 172

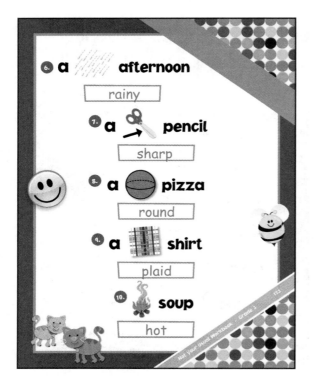

Page 173

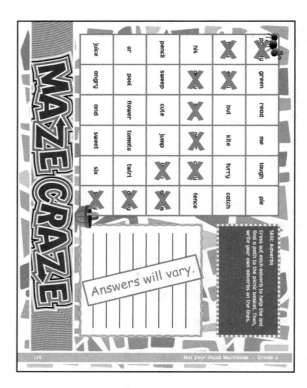

Page 174

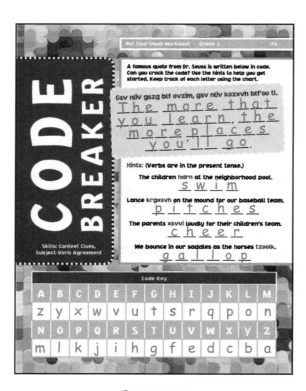

Page 175

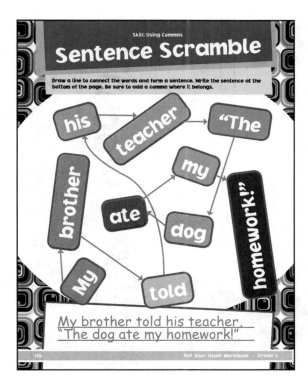

Page 176

Page 177

Page 178

Page 179

SUDOKU for you

F	C	R	E	**O**
E	O	C	**F**	R
O	F	E	R	C
C	R	F	O	E
R	**E**	O	C	F

Skill: Vocabulary

Write letters in the spaces so that each row and column contains the letters to spell a five-letter word that means "a push or a pull." No letter should appear twice in the same row or column. Do not guess. Use logic!

Write the word here:

<u>force</u>

Page 179

Page 180

JUMBLED UP

Skill: Spelling

SILHOUETTE

How many smaller words can you make from the letters in "silhouette"? Write the words on the lines.

Possible answers:

sit	holes
hot	silo
let	shout
sheet	shoe
teeth	shut
hut	louse
slit	heel
slot	
shot	
house	

Page 180

Page 181

hike   march
stroll   walk

Skills: Verbs, Vocabulary

IN PIECES

Synonyms are words that have the same or nearly the same meaning. Cut out the pieces. Put them together to make two separate squares containing verbs that are synonyms.

leap   spring
bound   jump

Page 181

Page 183

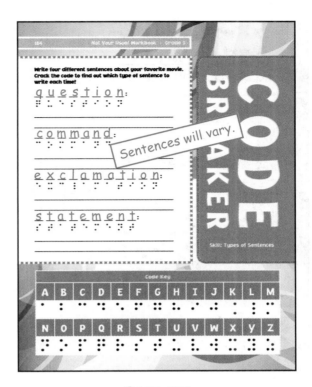

Page 184

Page 185

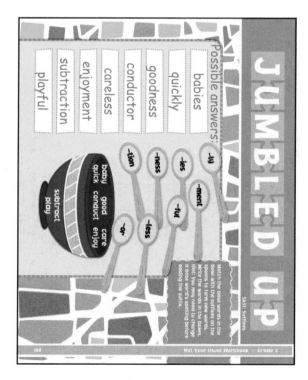

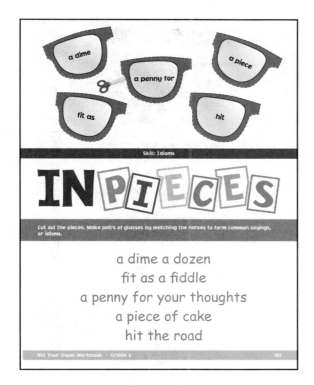

Page 189

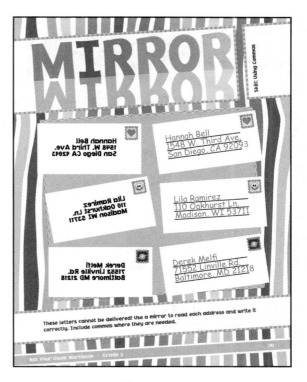

Page 191

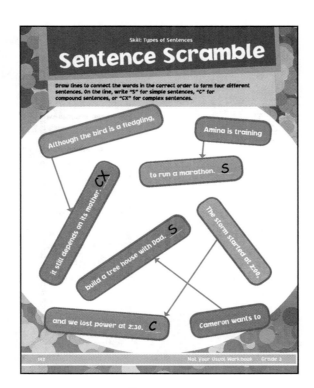

Page 192

Page 193

Page 194

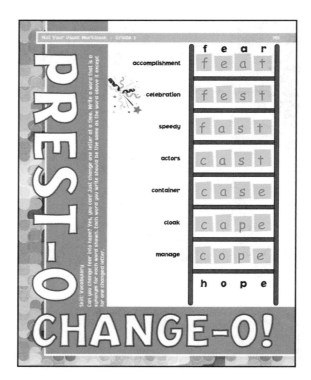

Page 195

Page 196

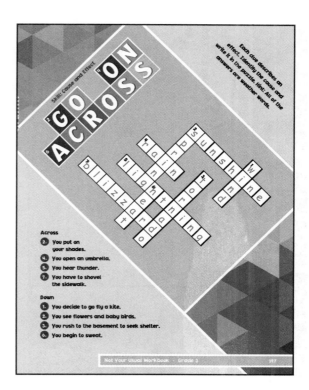

Page 197

Page 148

Page 199

Page 200

Page 201

Page 202

Page 203

Page 204

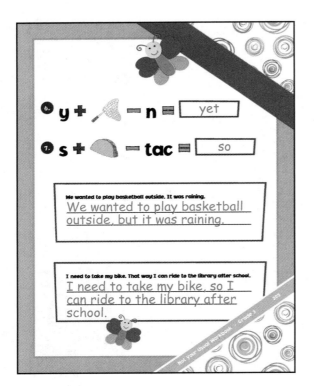

6. y + 🪤 - n = [yet]

7. s + 🌮 - tac = [so]

We wanted to play basketball outside. It was raining.
We wanted to play basketball
outside, but it was raining.

I need to take my bike. That way I can ride to the library after school.
I need to take my bike, so I
can ride to the library after
school.

Page 205

Sudoku for you

E	L	I	V	S
L	S	E	I	V
V	E	S	L	I
S	I	V	E	L
I	V	L	S	E

Skill: Plurals

Write letters in the spaces so that each row and column contains the letters to spell the plural form of "life." No letter should appear twice in the same row or column. Do not guess. Use logic!

Page 206